THE
FIRST

Frank Wedekind

THE FIRST

english version by
Eric Bentley

APPLAUSE
NEW YORK · LONDON

An Applause Original
THE FIRST "LULU"
English version by Eric Bentley of Frank Wedekind's PANDORA's BOX
(1892-4.)

Library of Congress Cataloging-in-publication data:
Wedekind, Frank, 1864-1918. [Büchse der Pandora. English]
    Frank Wedekind's The first Lulu / English version by Eric
    Bentley. p.   cm.
    "An Applause original."
    "English version ... of Frank Wedekind's Pandora's box."
    ISBN 1-55783-173-4   (pbk.) : $12.95
    I. Bentley, Eric, 1916- . II. Title. III. Title: First
    Lulu. PT2647.E26B8   1993
    832'.912—dc20   93-34202
    CIP

British Library Cataloging-in-publication data:
A catalogue record for this book is available from the British
Library

Applause Theatre Books, Inc.

211 West 71st Street	406 Vale Road
New York, NY 10023	Tonbridge KENT TN9 1XR
Phone: (212) 496-7511	Phone: 0732 357755
Fax: (212) 721-2856	Fax: 0732 770219

First Applause Printing, 1994

The First "Lulu" is dedicated to the memory of my friend and collaborator Hugo Schmidt (1929-1993).

—E.B.

CONTENTS

THE FIRST
"LULU"

Directed by
Robert Hupp

Dr. Franz Schoning, *a writer* ....Craig Smith
Edward Schwarz, *a painter* ....John Lenartz
Dr. Goll, *Dean of the Medical School*.......................T. Walker Rice
Lulu ....Elise Stone
Alva Schoning, *a playwright*............................Steve Chizmadia
Schigolch...Harris Berlinsky
Henriette, *a maid*...Kathleen Wilson
Countess Geschwitz....................................Adrienne D. Williams
Rodrigo Quast ....John Lynch
Ferdinand, *a butler*..Kennedy Brown
Madelaine de Marelle ....Kathleen Wilson
Bianetta Gazil..Sandra Sciford
The Marquis Casti-Piani ....T. Walker Rice
Puntschuh, *a banker*.....................................Kennedy Brown
Kadéga di Santa Croce ....Monique Vukovic
Bob, *a domestic* ....Thomas Donnarumma
1st customer ....Craig Smith
2nd customer ....Michael Anduz
3rd customer..John Lynch
4th customer..John Lenartz

Set Design by   Costume Design by   Lighting Design by
Jim Lartin-Drake   **Susan Soetaert**   **Giles Hogya**

Original Music by   Production Manager
Ellen Mandel   **Patrick Heydenburg**

THE FIRST "LULU"
Nine Notes

by Eric Bentley

FRANK WEDEKIND: A CHRONOLOGY

1863:   Conceived in Oakland, California.

1864:   Born in Hannover, Germany.

1872:   The Wedekind family moves to Switzerland: *Spring's Awakening* will reflect Wedekind's schooldays there.

1891:   *Spring's Awakening* published but not produced.

1892.   While in Paris, starts writing his *Lulu* play.

1894:   After a visit to London, the *Lulu* play is completed.

1898:   The first three acts of this play plus one new act are produced under the title *Earth Spirit:* Wedekind, under a pseudonym, plays the role of Schoning. *The Tenor* is produced.

1899-1900: Wedekind imprisoned (for insulting the Kaiser).

1901:   Wedekind performs in cabaret (The Eleven Hangmen). *The Marquis of Keith* is produced.

1904:   The last two acts of his original *Lulu* play plus one new act are produced under the title *Pandora's Box.* Thus, the play has now become two plays and will be best known in this form until 1988. For the two-play version, Wedekind did much re-writing.

1905:   A historic evening. *Pandora's Box*, which can be performed only "privately" for invited guests is produced by the great Viennese littérateur, Karl Kraus: Wedekind as Jack, Kraus himself as Kungu Poti, Tilly Newes (later Wedekind's wife) as Lulu.

1906:   *Spring's Awakening* is at last produced, though much cut. Max Reinhardt is the director. In the cast are Moissi, Eysoldt and, Wedekind's favorite, Albert Steinrück.

1906-1918:   Wedekind had considerable success acting in his own plays, especially *Hidalla*. As a playwright, he ended writing some rather conventional drama, three of them in praise of strong men of history or legend whom he admired—Hercules, Samson and Bismarck.

1914:   With most of Germany's leading writers, he expressed enthusiasm in print for the Kaiser's war. Later, he remarked, "Sometimes one has to howl with the wolves," and wrote some anti-war verses. Appendicitis, which he developed in 1914, seems never to have been satisfactorily dealt with by the doctors, and he died in 1918. His funeral in Munich (reported by Brecht and others) was almost taken over by a crowd of prostitutes, his devoted fans.

Only from 1918 on were restrictions lifted on the right to perform *Pandora's Box*. Even the G.W. Pabst film of 1928 is much bowdlerized. At his death in 1935, Alban Berg had all but finished his opera, *Lulu*, but his widow would not allow it to be completed by others: release from this ban had to await her death in 1978.

1988:   The German theatre magazine *Theater Heute* publishes the original one-play version of the *Lulu* story.

1989:   Peter Zadek directs the world première in Hamburg.

1991:   The Jean Cocteau Repertory Company and Applause Theatre Books jointly commission Eric Bentley to provide the American version.

1992:   Edward Bond and Elisabeth Bond-Pablé write a British version and have it produced.

1993:   Eric Bentley writes *The Wedekind Cabaret*, an entertainment made up of approximations in English of Wedekind's poems and songs. Music by William Bolcom and Arnold Black.

FRANK WEDEKIND'S ANSWERS

(to a list of queries in the notebook of a colleague)

Favorite quality in a man?	Temperament. Energy.
Favorite quality in a woman?	Intelligence.
Your idea of happiness?	Being used up, in line with one's disposition.
What are you cleverest at?	Lying.
Uncleverest?	Telling the truth.
Favorite academic field?	Theology.
Direction in art?	Michelangelo, Titian, Rubens, Makart.
Favorite kind of company?	Easygoing, amusing.
Unconquerable aversion to?	Tinkling away at the piano.
Favorite writer?	Schiller.
Favorite composer?	Beethoven.
Favorite book?	Casanova's *Memoirs*.
Favorite instrument?	String quartet.
Favorite literary hero?	Richard III.
Favorite historical hero?	Alexander the Great.
Favorite sport?	Acting.
Favorite game?	The game with the world.
How do you live?	After a fashion.
Temperament?	Melancholy.
Chief characteristic?	I hope: pigheadedness.
Motto?	2 times 2 equals 4.

THE LULU MORITAT

(To be sung to the tune of "She Was Poor But She Was
Honest")

She was born in the big city
In the middle of a slum
Chap called Shig passed for her papa
And a harlot was her mum.

And when she was six or seven
Gent called Shunning and no fool
Washed her, dressed her, combed her, groomed her
Placed her in a classy school.

At sixteen or maybe sooner
She was Shunning's joy and pride.
Did we tell you he was married?
He had Lulu on the side.

Set her up too with a husband
Doc of Med'cine name of Goll.
When the doc was at the clinic
She was Frankie Shunning's moll.

Dr. Goll, he hired a painter
Name of Quartz or Schwartz or so
He would capture Lulu's beauty
On his canvas, make it glow.

Oh these painters with their models!
Always get them into bed.
That's what Schwartsy did with Lulu.
When he found out, Goll dropped dead.

Lulu got his dough, and Schwartsy
He got Lulu for a wife.
He was oh so very happy
Tell he heard about her life.

Shunning's first wife died and Shunning
Had a second wife in view
Wished to be so faithful to her
That he'd have to drop Lulú.

After all, she had a husband,
What need Shunning on the side?
But when Schwartsy got the message
He committed suicide.

What an awkward situation!
Shun can't marry like he said.
No, he's gonna knuckle down and
Marry our Lulú instead.

Shunning had a son called Alva
(After Thomas Edison).
On the wedding day our Lulu
Went to bed with Shunning's son.

Shun became a morphine addict
And then with his ev'ry breath
He resolved to end the story
With the lovely Lulu's death.

Lulu's death! Should Shunning kill her?
If he did so, he'd be through.
He must chat with her, persuade her
She herself the deed must do.

Or must she? The lovely Lulu
Gamely gave Shun's plan a try.
Made her want to go on living.
It was Shunning who must die!

She put one, two bullets in him—
Newspapers would call it three—
Then to 'scape police and prison
Ran away to Gay Paree.

In Montmartre lovely Lulu
Found a house of much ill fame.
Alva Shun was now her husband.
Countess D'Oubra was her name.

In Paree had many lovers
One, a famous Fancy Man
Posed as an Italian Marquis.
He too had a little plan:

Lulu now would move to Cairo
Scene of Oriental lore
And in a luxurious whorehouse
She would be a luxury whore.

"Fuck with ev'ry man that pays me?
No, no, no, that is not me!"
"I'll tell the cops you murdered Shunning
If you don't at once agree!"

Now the fat is in the fire!
What can lovely Lulu do?
This time she don't have no money
Only has, as helpers, two:

Alva and her father Shiggy
(If this rascal *is* her dad)
All three of them flee to London:
See what there can now be had.

Cold and broke, all three are starving
But says Shig (still full o'fun):
Let the now unlovely Lulu
Walk the streets of Albion!

'Twas the time of Jack the Ripper
Exact dates not known to us
But we know he butchered prosties
And cut out the uterus.

On the first and last occasion
Lu agreed to play the whore
Her first john said: let's get filthy!
Lu said: moi, je fais l'amour.

Second john was—dare we say it?
Second john—O world take note!
Second john—how shall we play it?
Second john—he cut her throat.

Was it Jack? There is no knowing.
Jack remains a mystery.
That her uterus was missing
Cops and medicos agree.

And that night another girl was
Butchered by the butcher man.
It was she who most loved Lulu
Countess Gesh, the Lesbian.

MORAL

Lovely ladies, man adoring,
Learn from lovely Lulu's fate:
Don't decide to go out whoring
When the Ripper's at the gate.

HE'S BRECHT BUT HE'S ALSO SCHILLER

In the 1990s, many students will examine the differences between the first and the later *Lulu*, and some will find the later version preferable. Wedekind himself wrote, at one point, of having made many improvements in the script. The changes were not confined to softenings of the text that might help him get past the censors. *The First "Lulu"* is untidy, and would undoubtedly have been pruned and polished had Wedekind ever prepared it for a production.

Some of us prefer *The First "Lulu"* however, not because it contains all the raw and raunchy bits that could never have passed the censors of those days, but because it is superior in style and structure. Conversely, what Wedekind and others may have seen as an improvement in the revised text, was not that, but only an adjustment to a more conventional type of theatre.

It helps to look at Wedekind's career as a whole. Few writers, even the greatest, just get steadily better. What they hope for is a meaningful development, preferably without a decline. Wedekind's writing career does, however, show a decline, not so much a weakening from within as a retreat resulting from decisions deliberately taken. He was tormented by his experiences of the 1890s: production of *Spring's Awakening* postponed indefinitely as it then seemed, *Lulu* needing endless readjustments. He felt capable of writing a dramaturgically more orthodox kind of masterpiece and came up with *The Marquis of Keith*. It got an immediate production but it was a flop. "Orthodoxy" had not paid off. The thought of being misunderstood and unappreciated became the man's obsession and came to dictate what he would write. And he wrote *about* being misunderstood and unappreciated. He went on stage—to *be* the misunderstood, unappreciated artist. I for one would give anything to have seen him play himself, as he did over 100 times in *Hidalla*: as an ensemble of effects it was riveting theatre. The text, without his presence in the flesh, is something else again. I think several of his hitherto neglected plays will be revived. Many will not. *Lulu*, in one version or another, is his supreme achievement. *Spring's Awakening* comes in a good second. These two plays were original. Perhaps leaning a little on Büchner, Wedekind here invents what Brecht would call Epic Theatre, rejecting well-carpentered three- or four-act structures, and featuring an Elizabethan open form. His own special contribution to this form was that in both of these plays, the very mode of the discourse changes imperceptibly from the white light of everyday to the lurid tints of a higher reality—if not higher, anyway, the reality of nightmares and hallucinations.

That is where *Spring's Awakening* transcended by so much the little tract on sex enlightenment for which it was mistaken. And the last scene of *The First "Lulu"* can be taken not only at face value but also as Lulu's nightmare. Just as the teachers of *Spring's Awakening* are seen through the eyes of the boys, so here the Four Johns are seen through her eyes: Venus here meets her antagonists and finds herself hated, rejected, defeated, cut to pieces.

In his anxiety to be better understood (for unlike some modernists he never enjoyed being misunderstood), Wedekind later elected to be less original. His originality had meant, for one thing, being markedly different from his rival, Gerhart Hauptmann, a master of the well-crafted three- or four-act structure. Alas, it was a structure that Wedekind reverted to both in his revised version of the *Lulu* play and in new plays like *The Marquis of Keith*.

Wedekind began as an Ibsenite, and we find him giving readings of Ibsen plays even after, as a playwright, he had rebelled against Ibsenism. The rebellion was not against the externals only of Ibsenite drama. Rather, his whole thrust was going to be different. Ibsen's way is to conceal violent secrets under a placid, respectable surface. Wedekind would show some of the respectable surfaces but would smash through them. And if this seems mainly an attempt to break through into a wilder, more modern mode, it is at the same time a reaching back to the high drama of Schiller, his favorite writer (Brecht's unfavorite). The whole modern movement at the time seemed to want theatrical dialogue to be conversational, colloquial. Wedekind wanted it to be Schillerian, magniloquent.

One technical feature of his narrative, in *The First "Lulu,"* is of special interest: a bizarre displacement of accent. Lulu married four times. We see no weddings and in Act Four are just told in passing, as if it hardly mattered, that Alva is now her husband. When we notice an accent withheld in this way, we ask what in this case does receive the accent. Answer: not any irruption from the distant past as in Ibsen. Possibly something far more trivial but of the present. Something that Wedekind would call the self-evident—whereby he disclaims Ibsenite access to deep secrets. His chosen motto was 2x2=4. On the analogy of Realpolitik, he called his version of human beings: Realpsychologie. Realpolitik was a politics that admitted—against all the claims of political rhetoric—that 2x2=4.

The Wedekindian method does not exclude all the effects of classic dramaturgy, though it is likely to *displace* them—to use, as it were, syncopation where one is used to a strong downbeat. A prime example is Reversal (peripeteia) in *The First "Lulu."* The big reversals in five act plays come in or around the fourth act. The big reversal in *The First "Lulu"* comes in Act Two, the initial exposition of plot barely complete, with Schoning's decision to remarry and throw Lulu over. Although he does not carry out that decision, nothing is the same again after he has announced it. The adulterous arrangement Schoning had made during his first marriage had established the only stability—a relative one, to be sure—that Lulu was ever to know. It could not be restored by Schoning's now agreeing to marry her. On the contrary. Marriage in this play always carries a negative sign. It is adultery that can sometimes carry a (small) plus sign. Thus, what in a conventional plot, would be marriage as a victory for Lulu, almost a happy ending, is here marriage as a sign of defeat. Schoning becomes a morphine addict, plots the death of Lulu, and himself ends up dead.

A five-act play that has its Big Reversal in Act Two must then spend three (in this case, very long) acts in movement downwards. Down, down, down! What Racine would polish off in half an hour Wedekind will spin out to two or three hours. Is he mad? No, because the downward movement is integral to his purpose, and *needs* this amount of time for its expression. Luckily, the Wedekindian method does not exclude an interweaving of plot elements not unknown to great drama of the past. Act Four, for example, is a technical *tour de force*. Here, with great lucidity, he writes, as it were, two chapters in the "Life and Adventures of Lulu"—the Casti Piani chapter and the Rodrigo-Geschwitz chapter—while adding a third chapter about Puntschuh and his Virgin Funicular shares and a fourth telling how a 12-year-old from a convent school became a whore in the course of a single day, here a single act.

This Epic Theatre—in the amplitude of five acts and many roles—can tell whole life stories, not just Lulu's. And these stories are not parallel and independent, they are interwoven with each other: the interweaving signifies not only plot but theme—is not just action, but action with emergent meaning. The only character besides Lulu who is in all five acts is Alva. In a first quick reading of the play you would hardly realize at times that he's around: he is a *weak* man. Dramatically, it proves that he is very much around, and each of his reappearances—in Acts Two, Three, Four, and Five—is a shock effect, so much is he, each time, changed from what he was before. The continued downward movement of the heroine in the last two acts is reinforced by the continued downward movement of Alva, seen in Act One as the successful avant-garde writer, seen in Act

Three as the brash, brazen lover of his father's wife.

For many, the most memorable character, outside of Lulu herself, in any version of this play, is the old man who may be her father, Schigolch. In the Pabst film, he came off only as comic relief. The brevity of the film and perhaps the insensitivity of its director deprived him of his place in the scheme of things. Wedekind had worked him carefully into both plot and theme. He is not just the lover of his (perhaps) daughter, in the telling of their story he is a foil to her. While we see Lulu use up the energies of a lifetime in a mere two or three years, until in the last act we are shown the contrast between the Pierrot painting, made when Lulu was 18, and the emaciated hooker she has now become, we are also getting a carefully articulated series of glimpses of Schigolch. He is already old and seemingly finished at the outset but in Act Five, when the others (Lulu, Geschwitz, Alva) are really finished, he is all set to be the sole survivor. As the attic where they are living becomes the scene of one murder after another, he slips downstairs to flirt with a barmaid. While the others court death and get it, he would seem to be achieving eternal life.

So much for Wedekind's virtuosity as a play maker. The primary appeal of *The First "Lulu"* does not stem from this complexity but from a certain simplicity—the simplicity of sheer, consecutive incident in a well-told tale, A followed by B, followed by C, and so on through the alphabet. This too is Epic Theatre. One would hardly suppose the play to be based on a dramatic plot—plot of *Hamlet*, plot of *Phèdre*. It is balladesque, and one has to think of the kind of ballad called by Germans a *Moritat* (Mord-tat), as in the "Moritat of Mackie Messer" that opens *The Threepenny Opera*. In the days before general literacy a ballad-singer with a hurdy-gurdy would hold up passersby to tell them the tale of the latest crimes and natural disasters. One would think *The First Lulu* had been based on some Lulu Moritat like the one I have printed above by way of plot summary.

PANDORA

There is no doubt that Frank Wedekind saw in Lulu a character of mythic proportions. He seems to have considered calling his play *Astarte* and did call it *Pandora's Box*. Consequently scholars have researched these mythic ladies and others and have come up with much rather interesting information about them. Frank Wedekind read widely, it is clear, but it is doubtful if his text really requires from us any such investigation into the recondite. Works which are extremely well known—and were certainly known to Wedekind—will provide just as firm an anchorage. For Wedekind the most important of models was always *Faust*, the play which not only proclaimed the Ewig-Weibliche (Eternal Feminine) but also impelled us to ask what on earth the Ewig-Weibliche can possibly be. Wedekind never claimed he had the answer but he never ceased to reiterate the proclamation and in some sense, Goethean or not, he affirmed the principle which, whatever else it is, is certainly the opposite of misogyny.

If Lulu has mythological resonance, is she what a Wedekind title proposes—Pandora? Who, for that matter, *is* Pandora? One consults Robert Graves' book *Greek Myths*. In his sources, Graves finds that she was "as foolish, mischievous and idle as she was beautiful" and was "the first of a long line of such women." She opened a box belonging to her husband which was supposed to stay shut and it let out "the Spites" that plague mankind such as: "Old Age, Labour, Sickness, Insanity, Vice and Passion." Graves suggests that we either take the story as an anti-feminist fable or as a warning to males not to pry into female mysteries.

The first thing to understand about Wedekind's literary allusions, whether they are to ancient fable or to current works by Dumas *fils*, Wagner or Leoncavallo, is that they are invariably ironical—that is to say, an inversion of the established meaning is indicated even when, as with the Ewig-Weibliche, the established meaning is not flatly rejected. (On this last point he took his cue from his loved and resented Meister, Henrik Ibsen, who had already made such double allusion to the Ewig-Weibliche in *Peer Gynt*.) There is of course more than one way of making such inversions. They need not be made directly by the author. A positive statement can be negated by attribution to a negative character. So it is here with *Pandora*. The question to be asked is: to whom is Lulu a Pandora? Among the characters in the play, only two come into question. One is her last husband, Alva Schoning, who blames her for everything that has gone wrong. Yet he seems in this, something of special pleader. The one character who *acts* as if he considered her a Pandora, though he says nothing about it, is Jack—the Ripper.

WHO IS JACK? JUST A JOHN?

Obviously not the historical Jack the Ripper, if such a person existed. (A recent investigator concluded that the so-called Ripper murders were the fruit of a conspiracy and therefore not the work of a single man.) Not *any* Jack, one could conclude, as no name is attributed to this intruder in the play as staged. He is just the fourth and last of Lulu's "johns" on the first evening she walked the streets.

The question who is Jack? must here be coupled with the question, who is Lulu? The fifth and last act of *The First "Lulu"*—the act which got the goat of the Censors until 1918—lays out the subject and Frank Wedekind's conclusions methodically.

After her struggles of Acts One through Four, what is Lulu left with? Streetwalking. She has been called a whore from the beginning, but only now does she feel like one. Even now, she boggles. When the college instructor from Switzerland asks her to get "filthy" with him, she replies, "Moi, je fais l'amour," and when she ought to be listening carefully to what Jack is saying, she is actually telling him not to worry about having no money, she just wants him to stay with her all night. The action of the whole play culminates here. Here at last Lulu stands revealed as a romantic dreamer and idealist, far, far removed from the actuality under her very nose: Jack doing what he came there to do.

Which was what? What brought Jack to Lulu's attic? He talks as if he came as expected, for sex, and simply had to discuss the price and the length of his stay: lines about her attractive body, and especially her lips, can be taken as a logical part of this small enterprise. However, the murder he commits is not a Sex Murder, if this phrase denotes rape followed by homicide: it is a homicide that is itself a non-sexual form of rape—a symbolic mutilation—real mutilation, that is, which symbolizes a non-real rape. Thus Jack becomes, for Wedekind, the diametric opposite of Lulu. If she is Desire, and the Desire to be Desired, he is the embodiment of You-Can-Just-Say-No and say it with actions that carry not just the idea of rejection but loathing of the rejected object—fear of it too, the fear one might have of a rat or a snake till every ounce of life has been beaten out of it. If Wedekind's play were moved further towards the abstractness of Expressionism, one could just say Lulu is Woman, Jack is Misogyny, from which it would be but a step to: Lulu is Life, Jack is Death. As things are, both are individuals, but the larger forces certainly loom behind them. (When Lulu asks Jack if he is homosexual, she has sensed that the customary heterosexual electricity is absent from the scene.)

"Jack", or whatever his name is, kills Lulu and cuts out what we must assume is her uterus. And if Sex Murder is one misreading of this passage, there can be others. The playwright Edward Bond says—if I may paraphrase—that the whole play is about money and its relation to love and so we must believe "Jack" when he declares himself short of cash and we must also take it that he wants the uterus for the price it can presumably bring. Wedekind's text however—even in the translation by Bond and his wife—indicates that "Jack" will never try to turn this transaction into cash: money, he lets us know, will be collected only by his heirs when they sell this treasure to a Museum.

The misunderstanding is worth mentioning not only because Wedekind has always been a man people insist on misunderstanding but because, in this short passage, the significance of the whole play is at stake. In Bond's view (as faithfully as I can report it) the play is just a critique of the cash nexus, of capitalism. But since "Jack" is *not* going to sell the uterus what *is* he going to do with it? He is going to guard and treasure, it, taking it out from time to time—perhaps on certain days, at a certain hour—to gaze at and thereby to gain mystical insight into, who knows? the universe? Meanwhile there are other women to kill, other uteruses to be excised.

In many ways, the two masterpieces of Wedekind's youth, *Spring's Awakening* and *The First "Lulu,"* make a pair, not least in their quite unconventional and surprising final scenes. *Spring's Awakening* is surprising in its whole structure since the mode of the writing changes as the play proceeds from relatively naturalistic dialogue to episodes that a later generation would call expressionistic—where the schoolteachers et al. are heard and seen through the ears and eyes of children—and on from there to a scene of philosophic fantasy in which the protagonist (Melchior-Wedekind) is confronted by a Moritz who presents the case for withdrawal from life and by a Masked Man (Nietzsche-Wedekind)* who presents the case for living on, come what may. Such is the life-affirming ending to this story of (a) suicide and (b) death by botched abortion.

The ending of *The First "Lulu"* is parallel. "Jack" is another Masked Man—one has no idea who this chap may be—but where the earlier figure was the life force, this one is the death force, yet not in a blandly general sense as in some medieval morality that reminds us that we *all* die. No, he is the death *bringer*, and the spot he brings death to is our ultimate source: our mother's womb. One can appreciate how bitterly Frank Wedekind resented being taken for a misogynist, for that is what his blackest villain is here: "Jack" is a "serial killer", not in wishing to kill after enjoying sex, but in wishing to kill sex, punish woman for her sexuality, and do his bit toward preventing the perpetuation of the human race. His attitude is religious fanaticism with a racial cleansing in prospect that would cleanse the whole planet of human beings.

And he makes an incidental killing of another woman in this scene, the woman whom both he and Lulu call a "monster"**, because she is a Lesbian. Since her womb is never going to harbor a child, "Jack" ought really not to bother. He kills her anyway: she is female and she is not asexual.

* In a note Wedekind identified Nietzsche, not with the Masked Man, but with Moritz. Another aspect of Nietzsche is thus invoked, an aspect perhaps better called Schopenhauer.

** What in this book is called *The First "Lulu"* was called by Wedekind *Pandora's Box: A Monster Tragedy*. Today, *Pandora's Box* would be a confusing title: for so many years it has been the title of the second play in the two-play version. As for the word "Monster," it is not clear to whom it applies. Noting this, the stage director Peter Zadek has suggested it may apply to Wedekind! In his text, it is applied only to Countess Geschwitz...

LESBIANS ON STAGE

Was Wedekind the first modern playwright to put homosexuality on stage? The first, anyway, of any notoriety. *Spring's Awakening* (1891) has a scene of homosexual love and one of (flight from) masturbation. *The First "Lulu"* (1892-4) presents Martha, Countess of Geschwitz, and, in a response to courts of law that had passed judgment on his work, we find Wedekind writing (in 1906) that the central figure of his tragedy is not Lulu but Geschwitz. Perhaps he wrote this mainly to underline the Christian compassion with which the Countess is treated, and indeed he makes her like another Marguerite Gautier in her willingness to vindicate herself by self-sacrifice. If the play is Lulu's, it's pagan; if it's Geschwitz's, it's Christian; and he is arguing here for a Christian play. We also find out from this Note of Wedekind's that he considered Lesbians to be burdened with the curse of abnormality (his language) and he pitied them because their spiritual struggles were bound to be "fruitless", by which I take it he means that they all, like Geschwitz, ask for love from those who cannot grant it (a strange assumption). All this helps to explain what, to readers in the 1990s, will seem the odd tone of Geschwitz's lines in the play: hers is a voice, especially in the last act, from beyond the fringe of what Wedekind would consider normality. Curiously, this has a marked dramatic value even for spectators who may be a little uncomfortable with it. Only Geschwitz in this play strikes a lyric, a poetic note, even though it be a wan, wailing, keening kind of poetry. Whatever the author's prejudices, it is a poignant irony that Geschwitz is the only person who could offer Lulu a love large enough for her needs. *Could* offer it; and does. She is not the central figure in the design but Wedekind does give her the last words of his script—and seems to have been a little uncertain what they should be. What if Geschwitz dies saying, "Oh, shit"? She had never talked like that before;

but one only dies once. If any actress can say, "Oh, shit," without making the audience giggle, after three and a half hours of *First "Lulu,"* it's a great curtain line.

HE'S NOT WAGNER AND HE'S NOT DUMAS *FILS*

For "Jack", Lulu is Pandora, and her uterus is Pandora's box, but this is only the perspective of one character (two, if one wishes to add Alva). Her four husbands see her differently, and indeed differently, too, from each other, as is clear from the nicknames they give her. For Dr. Goll, she is Little Nell, a small girl whom he can coop up in a not very heavily gilded cage, a dancing child, as much boy as girl. For the painter Schwarz, she is Eve. He can respond to her only if she seems to bring him her virginity: exiled from the Eden created by this fantasy, he kills himself. For Franz Schoning, she is Mignon, the mystery girl in Goethe's *Wilhelm Meister*. The word Mignon carries the connotation of a boy-lover, a Ganymede. There is also a sado-masochistic component: Schoning believes, though Lulu never confirms this, that she needs to be whipped. For Alva Schoning, Lulu is the object of incestuous love—his father's bride. He calls her Katya and perhaps sees her as an "exotic" Dostoyevsky character. One could go on and on, showing her to be a different woman for each of the other characters in the play. The Countess Geschwitz has her own clue to the secret of Lulu's appeal: that it is not limited to one sex but is pansexual.

So much for perspectives from within the play. Outside the play, perhaps the most significant context is the literature of prostitution. This, of course, as befitting the world's oldest profession, is vast. Rather than try—vainly—to contemplate it all, one might look at a representative work of 19th-century theatre: *La Dame aux Camélias* in prose drama; *La Traviata* on the operatic stage. The setting is bourgeois society in one of its simplest forms, and the moral assumptions made by the characters are the same as those made by contemporary audiences. Within this world, the prostitute is the Bad Woman (Woman as Bad Person) and the norms of the society are the laws of the Medes and Persians. *Camille*, as the Dumas play has been known in English, becomes dramatic because the woman cast as Bad is really Good: the whore with the heart of gold is a promiscuous body harboring the soul of a virgin. (The mind jumps forward to *Anna Christie* and other more recent items.) Within the ideology of the play, for a female to be sensual is wrong: that, as prostitute, she may also be venal is a lesser issue. What Dumas worked out for Marguerite Gautier is that the unfeminine vice of sensuality can be outweighed by the supremely feminine virtue of noble self-sacrifice, in which process she is also revealed as not at all sensual personally, just connected with a sensual profession. Also Dumas is kind enough not to ask Marguerite to live on in such a painful situation. He gives her terminal tuberculosis: a mercy killing.

Now there is no understanding Lulu without realizing that Wedekind has transvalued—or at least inverted—all these values. His fundamental proposition is that woman is not only permitted to be sensual—*she had better be*, or else her whole being will be perverted, as he considered the whole being of spinsterish suffragettes had been perverted. The point of view is naïvely expressed in a little poem of Wedekind's called (what else?) "Lulu":

Some people love a dog's life
It has regularity
I love the heaving seesaw
Of this world's raging sea.

Enduring science, living art,
Love is what I love:
Firstfruits of the earth below
Manna from heaven above.

If a man gives me the feeling
I'm strong, I'm splendid, I'm a success,
I'll jump for joy and, shouting,
Uncover my nakedness.

In the drama as Dumas *fils* understood and practiced it, the Bad Woman (bad because sensual) was confronted by at least one Good Man (good because upholding social stability, not least through the institution of marriage). Thus when Wedekind stands the Dumas heroine on her head, he has to tackle also the men—the society—that confronted her.

In his early youth, Wedekind may have imagined for a while that he could avoid this confrontation. An early unfinished work called *The Solar Spectrum* finds him toying with the idea of an erotic utopia in which the phrase "daughters of joy" would not be ironic. He noted that in Roman times, prostitutes sometimes were priestesses, and vice versa. In these circumstances, the word prostitute does not mean sex-for-money, it means sex as entertainment, even as art—with professionals in charge in a garden of earthly delights.

But *The Solar Spectrum* was not finished, and when *Spring's Awakening* and *The First "Lulu"* were finished, the Innocent Eros which indeed they celebrated was shown with a formidable antagonist: the power structure of modern society, in the form of school teachers, or in the form of leaders in the professions and in business, respectable and otherwise. If to Dumas *fils*, society was right, and disreputable women were wrong, to Wedekind, society is wrong, and disreputable women are not disreputable. He is the playwright of a sexual revolution.

But not naïvely so. For Lulu (I return now to her character) is not good in the conventional sense—as Dumas' Marguerite Gautier turns out to be, and as Brecht's Marguerite Gautier—Shen Te—will be in his *Good Woman of Setzuan*. She is beyond *that* good and evil, her goodness consisting in the fact that her sensuality is in itself innocent and even beautiful. But it cannot cut itself off from the unbeautiful and far from innocent aspects of life. Lulu will not only be confronted with evil in her antagonists. To fight them she will herself cease to be innocent. It's a jungle out there: among murderers, Lulu twice commits murder. To come out on top or even to come out alive, she might have had to commit other murders. Instead, she *is* murdered. The prospects for a liberated woman in a society that still wants its women subjugated or dead are not very good.

Is that the main thrust of *The First "Lulu"*? Or is the main thrust not, rather, its exhibition of Lulu—an alternative to all the Marguerite Gautiers and Shen Te's? An alternative also to strong heroic women like Shaw's *Saint Joan*—strong not least because, like Queen Elizabeth I, she is above or beyond sex? If Lulu is not (for most of us) Pandora, she is, I think for all of us, Venus and this too is best seen in the immediate 19th century context. If Wedekind stood Marguerite Gautier on her head, he did the same with the great Venus of that era, the Venus of Richard Wagner's *Tannhaüser*.

Like *La Traviata*, *Tannhaüser* presents a principal myth of its time. Virginity looms as a supreme virtue, and Venus, once the queen of true love, is, in a quasi-medieval setting, a demon, in contrast with the "pure" Christian Elisabeth. Wedekind's Lulu re-instates a queenly Venus and, if in the end she too partakes of the demonic, the source of the demonism is a would-be Christian society.

Capitalism! says Edward Bond; and, to be sure, money not only talks in this play, it controls many of the events. Not all, however. As noted above, the economic interpretation of history cannot account for what Jack is up to, nor indeed for the behavior of Lulu's husbands, one, two, three, and four. Wedekind is no Marxist. Rather, I'd say, a Dostoyevskian. Asked which Wissenschaft (science or field) most interested him, he replied, Religionswissenschaft.

FEMME FATALE?

When the first three acts of the *Lulu* play became (with one new act) the play *Earth Spirit*, the theatre had received a work which, unlike *The First "Lulu,"* culminated in husband-murder. This fact alone goes far towards explaining how Wedekind could ever have been considered a misogynist, and how Lulu could be considered just one of a swarm of demon ladies—man-killers all—in the literature of the *fin de siècle*.

But it also seems that Wedekind's viewpoint in these matters shifted somewhat in the 90s. In conversation, his daughter, Kadidja, gave me an account of this shift which is vivid in its simplicity. Wedekind, in the period concerned, had an affair with the estranged wife of Strindberg from which a son was born. Therewith Wedekind's viewpoint moved closer to the Strindbergian misogyny, making the Lulu of the revised, two-play version a more negative character than the first Lulu.

The point is strongly confirmed in the letter which Lulu, in the later version, has Schoning write to his fiancée calling off the wedding. This letter is actually dictated to him by Lulu, who has suddenly become the boss—the Lady Macbeth of "Infirm of purpose, give me the daggers!"—of which there is not a trace in *The First "Lulu."* Or look how the death of Schoning is handled in the two versions. The later one has Lulu emptying the barrel of the revolver with *five* bullets and continuing to pull the trigger after that. *The First "Lulu"* notes the firing of only *two* shots, one of which hits not Schoning, but Rodrigo: Schoning here is killed by a single shot, fired on a sudden impulse, and almost accidental.

It would seem that Wedekind was not wholly aware of the Strindbergian changes being wrought in his own work, for we find him blaming everything of this sort on the actress who first made the Lulu role famous in Berlin, and beyond: Gertrud Eysoldt (who not long before had played Salome, mankiller supreme.) In contrast, Tilly Newes, later Wedekind's wife, would play the role as he felt it should be played—offering a positive image of this Venus. He even described her performance, enthusiastically, as *Madonnenhaft*—madonna-like, a paradoxical compliment.

When Wedekind was dead, and censorship restrictions were lifted, the stage directors took over. Erich Engel and Otto Falckenberg made their own adaptations of the dual text, and other directors used these. The *Lulu* play(s) was (were) also adapted to the silent screen. In two of five silent screen adaptations the Danish star Asta Nielsen continued the Eysoldt tradition, or so I would gather (I have not seen the films): and the *femme fatale* of the 19th century would now be identified as a Twenties Vamp—short for Vampire. The fifth of these films was directed by G.W. Pabst, and Marlene Dietrich wished to play Lulu in it. She too would have been in the Eysoldt mold and a Vamp. But Pabst chose for the role an American star (starlet?) already fixed in another mode, that of Flapper—sexy but not man-hating or even man-threatening.

Dietrich got to offer her *femme fatale* anyway in a film that was a spin-off, if not a rip-off, from *Lulu, The Blue Angel* (1930). Thus, it might be said, the whole world got to know Lulu in a vein that Wedekind disapproved of—and yet for which he became in large part responsible when he changed *The First "Lulu"* into the two plays, *Earth Spirit* and *Pandora's Box*.

To publish *The First "Lulu"* in 1993, as Applause Theatre Books is now doing, is not to unearth some discarded and superseded first draft. It is comparable, rather, to stripping away layer after layer of gaudy paint in order to reveal the beautiful oak paneling beneath.

ACT ONE: FRAU DOKTOR GOLL (Nelly.)

ACT TWO: FRAU SCHWARZ (Eve.)

ACT THREE: FRAU DOKTOR SCHONING* (Mignon, Katya.)

ACT FOUR: MADAME LA COMTESSE

ACT FIVE: FRAU ALVA SCHONING (Katya, Daisy.)

* In the original, there is an umlaut on the "O." This is here deliberately omitted, to give the English-speaking actor a name he can more easily pronounce.

Munich*, 1883. Dr. Franz Schoning, writer, and editor of the local newspaper, has commissioned a portrait of his wife, recently deceased.

---

* Wedekind does not indicate which German city is the site of his first three acts, and at the time he wrote this play he had not lived long in any part of Germany. Munich is the city he would later be closely associated with.

CHARACTERS

Lulu:
Countess Geschwitz

Lulu's four husbands:
Dr. Goll
Schwarz, a painter
Dr. Franz Schoning, writer
Alva Schoning, playwright

Among Lulu's lovers:
Rodrigo Quast
The Marquis Casti-Piani
Schigolch (who may also be her father.)

People of Lulu's circle in Paris:
Madelaine de Marelle
Kadéga di Santa Croce
The Banker Puntschuh
The Journalist Heilmann
Bianetta Gazil
Ludmilla Steinherz

Domestics in Paris:
Bob
Armande

Lulu's four customers in Whitechapel:
Mr. Hopkins
Kungu Poti
Dr. Hilti
Jack

Briefly seen are:
Bernstein, a doctor
Ferdinand, coachman turned butler
A plainclothesman
and a crowd of gamesters in Paris

ACT ONE

Artist's studio, spacious,—Back left, main entrance. Front left, side door to the bedroom. Somewhat left of center at back, a platform. Behind the platform, a Spanish screen. In front of the platform, a Smyrna carpet. At front, on the right, two easels. On the one further upstage, in a provisional frame, the pastel portrait of a forty year old lady dressed for a ball. Against the other one, a canvas is leaning, the unpainted side on view. Left, several chairs. In front of the easels, an ottoman with Turkish cushions: a tiger's skin has been thrown over it, In the background, a high stepladder. The studio window is thought of as being an extension of the fourth wall. Afternoon.

SCENE ONE. Edward Schwarz. Dr. Franz Schoning.

SCHONING: (*A photo in his hand, he is examining the pastel portrait.*) I can't tell you just what it is, Herr Schwarz. I miss the very thing I wanted to have painted. This is certainly a lady dressed for a ball—but I don't find the human being I've looked up to half a lifetime with childlike reverence.

SCHWARZ: Working from a photo is not much fun, Dr. Schoning.

SCHONING: She could never bring herself to sit for a portrait. What was her phrase? "A glorification of the passing moment." Such homage to her own person! Well, she was too much the wife, too much the mother, to see it. —Do *you* see any of this in your painting?

SCHWARZ: Do you see any of this in the photo?

SCHONING: A hint, yes. —I remember telling *her* so. Oh dear, it's quite possible the memory of it all is just too vivid.

SCHWARZ: Your every word on the subject has been sacred to me. I've wandered through the streets in search of a human being to match the image in my head. Seeking a few points of contact with the reality.

SCHONING: (*Looking at the canvas.*) Maybe it's right. I don't know. As I say, I'm the worst judge. Anyone who knew her *less* well would recognize her at first glance.

SCHWARZ: How'd you like her hair, Dr. Schoning?

SCHONING: It's right. Just right. How delicately you've made the left hand stand out from the dress! You've changed the lighting.

SCHWARZ: The concept is borrowed from a little dancer at the Odeon..

SCHONING: (*Pointing to the photo.*) See this look on her face? Just below her forehead? Imagine she's talking to you, Herr Schwarz—she raises her brows—lowers her head—her eyes seem to break free. A being not of the senses only. A *higher* being. Nothing trivial, nothing *low* can come near her. Passing comprehension. All this in those luminous eyes, in that indefinably tranquil closed mouth.

SCHWARZ: Stand back from it, way back.

SCHONING: (*Moving slowly backwards bumps into the canvas leaning against the downstage easel.*) Sorry...

SCHWARZ: (*Picking the frame up.*) Don't worry...

SCHONING: (*Taking note of the picture.*) What—what...?

SCHWARZ: You know her?

SCHONING: No. Is she sitting to you?

SCHWARZ: Has been since Christmas. (*He lifts the picture on to the easel. A girl dressed as Pierrot. A tall shepherd's crook in her hand.*) There's an awful lot still missing.

SCHONING: And, um, that costume?

SCHWARZ: Does it surprise you? She has class, you know.

SCHONING: (*With a look at* SCHWARZ.) Then, er, congratulations!

SCHWARZ: Not at all...

SCHONING: Certainly.

SCHWARZ: Well, you know, her husband comes with her for the whole two hours. I have the pleasure of conversation with the old boy! About art, of course, just to consummate my happiness.

SCHONING: How did you get into this?

SCHWARZ: Dr. Goll comes tottering into my studio—fat dwarf of a man—do I want to paint his wife? Why wouldn't I? Even if she were ugly as night! Ten next morning. My door opens. The fat little pig propels this...Faery Child into the studio. I hold grimly on to my easel..At their heels, a punk in sap green livery with a parcel under his arm. —Where's the dressing room? —I open my bedroom door. Luckily the bed is made. The little sweetheart scurries in, the old man posts himself outside—a buttress, a bulwark! Two minutes later, out comes—Pierrot! (*Breathing hard.*) Magic! Fairy tale incarnate! At one with that impossible costume from top to toe, as if born in it! The way she raises her feet from the floor, buries her arms up to the elbows in her pockets, throws her small head to one side—so spontaneous! The blood shoots to *my* head!

SCHONING: In *your* profession, don't you get hardened against such attacks?

SCHWARZ: (*Shaking his head.*) Against *that*? And I'm disgusted when a model even bares her breasts.

SCHONING: So this is more than nudity?

SCHWARZ: Or less than nudity.

SCHONING: Differing perspectives then? Deeper ones? Equilibrium? The scales, even? I understand you. The soul evaporates in the heat, and then descends upon the body— as dew. The spirit inhabits the fig leaf!

SCHWARZ: I'll show you. One moment...(*Off, left.*)

SCHONING: (*Alone, to himself.*) This fellow needs to get out—out into the open!

SCHWARZ: (*Comes back with a white satin costume.*) I believe she wore this at the fancy dress ball.

SCHONING: (*Admiringly.*) Hmmm!

SCHWARZ: (*Unfolding the costume.*) Cut out in front and behind.

SCHONING: Gigantic pompons!

SCHWARZ: (*Feeling the pompons.*) Black silk.

SCHONING: Ravens in the snow!

SCHWARZ: (*Holding the costume up by the shoulder straps.*) She wears no corsets under this.

SCHONING: All in one piece...

SCHWARZ: Bodice and trousers.

SCHONING: No corsets, no stays...

SCHWARZ: She doesn't need them.

SCHONING: How does she get into it?

SCHWARZ: From the top.

SCHONING: Of course.

SCHWARZ: She has nothing else on.

SCHONING: When that thing glides off her shoulders...

SCHWARZ: Control yourself.

SCHONING: But it can't possibly stay up.

SCHWARZ: She stretches up her right arm.

SCHONING: But the long tubular legs—

SCHWARZ: They upset you?

SCHONING: They're *too* long.

SCHWARZ: She picks up the one on the left.

SCHONING: Yes.

SCHWARZ: That's her pose. She holds it in her hand just over her knee.

SCHONING: As if she had just peeled it off.

SCHWARZ: Delicious—how she does that.

SCHONING: The one on the right falls on her foot.

SCHWARZ: All the way forward to her toes.

SCHONING: And white satin shoes...

SCHWARZ: (*Sighing.*) And one has to get all this on to canvas.

SCHONING: Life is hard.

SCHWARZ: And there's also a coquetterie to it.

SCHONING: So admirable!

SCHWARZ: You can't imagine.

SCHONING: Au contraire. I see it.

SCHWARZ: (*Turning to the picture.*) Just look at this arm...

SCHONING: How elegantly she stretches it out!

SCHWARZ: She holds the shepherd's crook at the highest point she can reach.

SCHONING: Which raises her...chest.

SCHWARZ: And the armpit is completely uncovered.

SCHONING: Yes.

SCHWARZ: Many models would refuse.

SCHONING: Is it coquettish of her?

SCHWARZ: Hold on a minute. —The arm is a jewel. Facets. Every undulation producing its own accent. The elbow is a sort of armpit forced wide open as the arm straightens out. Behold the bright blue arteries. The delicate gleam and glamour. The shimmering of little lights.

SCHONING: I can imagine all that. I don't see it on your canvas.

SCHWARZ: Now about the armpit...?

SCHONING: Yes?

SCHWARZ: In the midst of strong mat flesh tone, it shows you two small locks of hair, burnished black.

SCHONING: They aren't there yet.

SCHWARZ: Of course she had them dyed.

SCHONING: How'd you arrive at *that* horrid suspicion?

SCHWARZ: Those locks are darker than the other body hair. Darker than the eyebrows. Whereas the body hair...

SCHONING: Keep going.

SCHWARZ: (*Folding up the costume.*) In any case she gave the matter a certain degree of conscious attention.

SCHONING: What I wanted to say...

SCHWARZ: Say it.

SCHONING: The old boy stands sentry?

SCHWARZ: As for me, you know—in general...(*He takes the costume back into the bedroom.*)

SCHONING: (*Alone, to himself.*) As for me—

SCHWARZ: (*Coming back, looks at the clock.*) Anyhow if you want to meet her...

SCHONING: No.

SCHWARZ: They'll be here any minute.

SCHONING: I'm content with the portrait. (*Turning to the pastel portrait.*) I'd be much obliged if you would design a frame for it.

SCHWARZ: As you wish, A few Immortelles...

SCHONING: I'll let your good taste decide. As I said...that picture has everything. Shall I see you at my place—soon?

SCHWARZ: (*Accompanying him.*) Thank you.

SCHONING: Stay where you are. (*Goes back left and runs into* DR. GOLL *and* LULU *at the doorway. Half to himself.*) In God's name.

SCENE TWO. Dr. Goll, Dean of the Medical School.*Lulu. The foregoing.

SCHWARZ: (*Hurrying over.*) May I introduce...

GOLL: (*Sizing* SCHONING *up.*) What are *you* doing here?

SCHONING: (*Giving* LULU *his hand.*) Frau Doktor Goll?

LULU: How very charming!

SCHONING: (*Shaking hands with* GOLL.) I was just looking at my late wife's portrait, Dr. Goll.

GOLL: I'm sorry then, um, Dr. Schoning.

LULU: You're not going to leave us, are you?

SCHONING: I was thinking...the sitting's about to begin?

LULU: That's just it.

GOLL: It's all right, stay.

SCHONING: You can't expect me to say no to that.

GOLL: (*Getting rid of hat and stick.*) Anyway I have to talk with you.

LULU: (*Giving her hat and coat to* SCHWARZ, *to* SCHONING.) Just

* In the German original, Dr. Goll is a fairly high medical officer in the state bureaucracy.

think, we were crossing the new bridge—down by the dockside—when who should drive by in her coach but the Duchess of Villa Franca.

SCHONING: And what might the Duchess have had on her mind?

GOLL: (*Contemplating the pastel portrait.*) She ought to have done more *living.* More living! —She had a good heart. (*Lighting a cigarette.*) Maybe the...stimulus was lacking.

SCHONING: Lacking to us all.

GOLL: Not to you, though.

SCHONING: One ought to *seek* stimulation. —What's wrong is that one doesn't. —One is too lazy. Too lazy even to go to sleep.

LULU: Why not upset the applecart?

SCHONING: The stimulus is lacking.

GOLL: Get going, Nelly: get dressed.

LULU: Now I'm in for it.

GOLL: Why else are we here? —Herr Schwarz is licking his paintbrushes.

LULU: Painting's his job. I always thought this might be more amusing.

SCHONING: At least you always have the satisfaction of giving pleasure to others.

LULU: (*Going left.*) Then just a moment...

SCHWARZ: (*Opening the bedroom door for her.*) If the Frau Doktor would be so kind...(*He closes the door behind her.*)

GOLL: Yes, I christened her Nelly.

SCHONING: Why didn't you call her Mignon?

GOLL: For me she's little Nell, the unfinished—the helpless—to whom a fatherly friend may not be dispensable just yet.

SCHONING: (*Lighting a cigarette.*) That way she doesn't have to be taken any too seriously.

GOLL: And knows better than to try to control her man.

SCHONING: While the advantages remain.

GOLL: Oh, I don't know about that. From dawn to dusk I have

the Grim Reaper to worry about. I've no children, you know. —One can't get rid of certain needs, however calcified one may become. (*To* SCHWARZ.) Tell me, what's with your little dancer friend?

SCHWARZ: She sat for me that time just as a favor. She was with the Saint Cecilia Choral Club when they came to town.

GOLL: (*To* SCHONING.) I think the weather will change.

SCHONING: I suppose getting into costume presents difficulties?

GOLL: Getting back into street clothes is more the problem. Has to be laced up, you know. Down her back. I'm the chamber maid.

SCHONING: You could invent some kind of rational dress for her?

GOLL: I like irrational dress too much. —(*Calling.*) Nelly!

SCHWARZ: (*Runs to the door and calls through the keyhole.*) Frau Doktor!

LULU: (*From within.*) Coming, coming!

GOLL: (*To* SCHONING.) He's an idiot. What to make of such people?

SCHONING: (*While* SCHWARZ *looks through the keyhole.*) I envy them. They possess their souls in peace. Evenings, guarding their treasure, they go quietly to sleep. You can't pass judgment on a fellow who's lived from palette to mouth since he was a kid. So don't. We'll make him rich instead.

LULU: (*Coming out of the bedroom as Pierrot.*) Here I come.

SCHONING: (*Taking note.*) Infernal!

LULU: (*Approaching.*) Well?

SCHONING: Takes my breath away.

LULU: You like me?

SCHONING: (*Overcome.*) Like you!

LULU: You see!

SCHONING: O my soul.

GOLL: A sight for sore eyes.

SCHONING: You've said it.

LULU: And *I* am fully aware of it.

SCHONING: Then you might be more human.

LULU: I do what I must do.

SCHONING: You used make-up.

LULU: I did NOT. But I may look like I have a sunburn!

SCHONING: On the contrary.

LULU: Under this snow white wig?

SCHONING: More blinding than ever.

GOLL: Her skin is uncommonly white. —I've told the artist, however, that FLESH should be in his thoughts as little as possible—also told him: Daubing is not painting!

SCHONING: Depends who does the daubing.

GOLL: If all you want is to paint cattle!

SCHWARZ: (*Busy at his easel.*) Anyhow, Impressionism solves more interesting problems than the sentimental crap of the Seventies.

SCHONING: There are two sides to everything.

SCHWARZ: YOU say that?

SCHONING: Two sides, yes, even to narrow-mindedness.

GOLL: (*To* LULU *who embraces and kisses him.*) Your chemise is showing, tuck it in, he's all set to paint it.

LULU: I should have taken it off, it's in the way. —(*Climbing on to the platform, to* SCHONING.) So, Dr. Schoning, what if YOU had to stand sentry for two hours...?

SCHONING: Me? —I'd give up my hopes of heaven to be such a creature as you!

GOLL: (*Sitting, left.*) Come over here. From here I find her even more beautiful.

LULU: (*Taking her pose.*) I'm equally beautiful from all angles. (*To* SCHWARZ, *with a turn of the head.*) A little *empathy*, please.

SCHWARZ: Right knee further forward—good. The satin costume is uniformly smooth and soft but always falls differently. —Today the lighting is at least bearable.

GOLL: Forget lighting. Hold the brush longer. —No impasto for her. She's not the super-colossal type.

SCHWARZ: I'm trying to get the expression down to just a few, so to say, moments.

SCHONING: Treat her as a still life.

SCHWARZ: Certainly.

GOLL: Art should delight the spirit. But today, when you go to an exhibition, the walls are covered with stuff that, at best, would make you castrate yourself.

SCHONING: (*Sitting beside him.*) What gets *you* to an exhibition in the first place?

GOLL: Just what I ask myself. Maybe the lousy weather.

SCHONING: The little O'Murphy girl is making her debut in the National Circus.

GOLL: As a pearl fisher from Peru. Prince Polossov took me to see her.

SCHONING: The biggest pearl in her catch!

GOLL: His beard has turned black again from sheer joy.

SCHONING: She'll break with him and take up with Anton.

GOLL: Or with a circus clown. What pigs they all are!

SCHONING: Do *you* find her so fabulous?

GOLL: I?

SCHONING: As those "pigs" do?

GOLL: No.

SCHONING: I've not seen her yet.

GOLL: Who's to judge?

SCHWARZ: (*Painting, now and then stepping back.*) I should've moved to another studio last Fall. But the idea of a move scared me. And when the sun comes up, the wall round the courtyard does throw warm rays in here.

GOLL: (*To* LULU.) What are you digging in your pockets for?

LULU: They're empty.

SCHONING: (*To* GOLL.) Did you think you'd left your handkerchief there?

SCHWARZ: The heating system also leaves something to be desired. The air is so dry in winter you get a headache later in the day.

GOLL: You've got to open a window! Nothing healthier than a fire in the grate and open windows!

SCHWARZ: (*Speaking to the other side of the room.*) Fireplace with a spit, a barbecue!

GOLL: (*To* SCHONING.) I think our opera house is on to something right now.

SCHONING: I don't believe it.

GOLL: Go see.

SCHONING: Not on your life.

GOLL: There's no hope for you. You're gonna come to a bad end...

SCHONING: Who's gonna come to a good end?

GOLL: Go to the opera. That's my prescription.

SCHONING: I'm taking chloral hydrate.

GOLL: Drop it. Take opera instead, it won't ruin your stomach or go out of fashion so fast.

SCHONING: So when is *she* dancing?

GOLL: Dancing? O'Murphy? She's singing.

SCHONING: Singing now?

GOLL: (*Singing from Act 2 of Tannhäuser.*) "Wolfram von Eschenbach, beginne!"

SCHONING: Tannhäuser. Four little boys sing that.

GOLL: But four little girls sing the parts.

SCHONING: You are the perfect Wagnerite. (*Singing from the same scene.*) "Könnt Ihr der Liebe Wesen mir ergründen? Wer es vermag...*

LULU: (*Interrupting.*) There's someone at the door.

SCHONING: (*Stopping singing.*) Oh excuse me. (*He goes to the door.*)

GOLL: (*Speaking to* LULU *about* SCHWARZ.) It's all right to smile

---

* "Love—can you get to the bottom of it for me? He who can do this..." This line is not quoted by Wedekind but it helps an American reader or spectator know why he has brought in Act 2 of Tannhäuser at all. Wagner and Nietzsche provide a background for Wedekind's treatment of love in this Act (in Act 3, Pagliacci is pointedly cited).

for him, he doesn't mind, what else are they for, such lips as yours all sugar and spice...Any aspersions would be on me.

SCHONING: (*Over his shoulder.*) Sugared Almonds! Strawberries and cream!

GOLL: Kid stuff, all that—

SCHONING: But then kids are your thing.

SCENE THREE. Alva Schoning. The foregoing.

ALVA: (*Still behind the Spanish screen.*) Is it possible for a friend of the Muses to...

SCHONING: You.

LULU: It's Alva Schoning.

GOLL: Well, let's take a look at you.

ALVA: (*Coming forward, giving* GOLL *his hand.*) How are you, Dr. Goll?

GOLL: Now don't be scared...

LULU: Alva Schoning has seen models before now.

ALVA: (*Turning suddenly around.*) My God!

LULU: you recognize me?

ALVA: Who that ever had a chance to admire you could forget you?

GOLL: (*To* SCHONING.) Pity you weren't present.

SCHONING: I'm in mourning, you see.

ALVA: (*To his father.*) How are you, father?

SCHONING: Fine. And you?

ALVA: I came over to take you to the dress rehearsal.

SCHONING: That's today?

LULU: Sunday's the opening.

GOLL: What's this? How would YOU know?

LULU: You read it out to me—from the paper.

GOLL: (*To* ALVA.) Tell me, my young friend, what's it called, this play of yours?

ALVA: Zarathustra.

GOLL: Zarathustra! I thought he was in the madhouse.

SCHONING: You're thinking of Nietzsche.

GOLL: Right. I always confuse them.

ALVA: I did take my material from his books.

SCHONING: It takes talent to make a cripple dance.

GOLL: Your play is a dance?

ALVA: Nietzsche, forgive me, is the greatest dance genius the world has ever seen.

GOLL: This must be *another* Nietzsche.

ALVA: Heavens, no!

GOLL: I thought he was a philosopher.

SCHONING: He thought the whole world limped. That made him dance for joy.

ALVA: You know him?

SCHONING: I find him repulsive. Hopping around like that cripple of his on crutches. I'd never base a ballet on his work.

GOLL: I don't get it.

SCHONING: We can all go crazy!

GOLL: Go crazy and dance!

ALVA: I made my whole second act out of his Dance Song. Girls on the greensward in the woods. The god Eros sleeping at the fountain. Zarathustra steps out of the bushes with his disciples. Dew falls.

GOLL: Well, well. Who did the music?

ALVA: I did. The first act takes place in the city called the Colored Cow. You see the tightrope walker. You see the young and old little women—

GOLL: Not bad—hm...

ALVA: You see the wild dogs, the crooked authorities, the little girls.

GOLL: Little girls?

ALVA: You see the last man, the red judge, the grunting pig, the pale criminal, the famous sage, the desert's daughters, the night watchman...

GOLL: The greatest ballet ever!

ALVA: ...and Zarathustra burying the blood-soaked rope-dancer in the market place at nightfall.

GOLL: That's Realism, I'm all for it! —Congratulations!

ALVA: Had problems with the third act. The best part is the scene where the fire mountain spits out the firedog and all the hobgoblins. The hobgoblins are in dark sacks from the waist up. You see nothing but legs...

GOLL: Legs—legs—therein lies the secret of great theater! —

ALVA: In the last act, they're upside down.

GOLL: (*Continuing his previous speech.*)—the humanity—the very spirit of theater!

ALVA: Fourth act—Zarathustra's homecoming—transformation scene—Zarathustra pulls the serpent from the shepherd's jaws—birth of Superman! La Corticelli dances that part with such grace...

GOLL: There was always something superhuman about her.

SCHONING: She's had a life. While her mother lived, she danced with her legs. On her own, she danced with her head. Today she dances with her heart.

GOLL: (*To* ALVA.) I hope you haven't thrown any dark sack over HER?

ALVA: Over Nietzsche's Superman?! She's to wear nothing. Or so as little as the police require.

GOLL: God be thanked.

ALVA: Which does not make her a superman.

GOLL: Hm...

ALVA: Superman, my dear doctor, has wings and curly hair. Frilly ruff around the neck. But it's what's below the ruff that counts if we're to reproduce and go, not just forward, but up. How are we going to put all that on stage?

SCHONING: My boy, beware the madhouse.

GOLL: Hm—is Corticelli rehearsing with the others?

ALVA: Everybody together—wild dogs, hobgoblins, little girls—décolletées down to their souls—the crooked authorities, the grunting pig—

GOLL: You're my guy.

ALVA: Then join us.

GOLL: I can't.

SCHONING: We must be going.

ALVA: Come with us, Doctor. In the last act, you'll see Zarathustra at his cave with the eagle, the serpent, the two kings and the old pope.

GOLL: I'm only interested in Superman.

ALVA: Then come. You'll love the donkey festival—that's the final scene...

GOLL: I can't, I can't.

ALVA: Why not? We'll stop by at Peter's Place and you can enthuse over Corticelli.

GOLL: Will SHE be there? At Peter's Place?

ALVA: The whole gang'll be there.

GOLL: Don't keep pushing me!

ALVA: You'll not be missing anything.

GOLL: No? When I get back, this fool will have messed up the picture.

ALVA: Oh, he can paint over it.

SCHONING: He's in no great hurry.

GOLL: No, next time, gentlemen.

LULU: Reserve a box for us, Sunday.

SCHONING: Of course, of course.

ALVA: (*Taking his father's arm.*) The desert's daughters are getting dressed...

GOLL: This damn daubing—you gotta explain every brush stroke to such people!

ALVA: Bye now, Frau Doktor.

LULU: Tell us about it later.

GOLL: Use my coach.

SCHONING: Thanks, we'll send it back.

GOLL: (*To* ALVA.) Greet the desert's daughters for me!

ALVA: They'll only bawl us out for not bringing you with us.

GOLL: But if this fellow gives Nelly a potato nose!

SCHONING: It's not the worst that could happen.

GOLL: Hm...Well...

SCHONING: I guarantee everything!...

ALVA: Let's go.

GOLL: (*Yielding, to* LULU.) I'll be back in five minutes.

ALVA: The desert spreads...

GOLL: (*Taking hat and stick.*) And I probably won't go to Peter's Place.

SCHONING: (*To* LULU.) Bye now.

ALVA: (*Also to* LULU.) Keep, oh, so still. (GOLL *and* SCHONING *rush to the door.*) The desert spreads—woe to the man who has deserts inside him! (*Leaves with the other two.*)

SCENE FOUR. Schwarz. Lulu.

LULU: He's not been leaving me alone for a minute.

SCHWARZ: (*Painting.*) Wouldn't you like a rest?

LULU: I'm afraid that...

SCHWARZ: None of my models keep still so long.

LULU: He can come back any time.

SCHWARZ: Hm—With us up north the ever-leaden sky—hardly ever a thunderstorm beneath—Down south the bright, warm gleam of the sun—but always a smell of decay—

LULU: I would never have imagined it.

SCHWARZ: Twixt north and south, hard to make a choice!

LULU: Better to have no choice.

SCHWARZ: What would you never have imagined?

LULU: That he might go with them.

SCHWARZ: Sour apples, rotten apples!

LULU: Paint.

SCHWARZ: Oranges won't grow in the north. A little stiffer on your left side. Enough!

LULU: I could stand here half my lifetime.

SCHWARZ: (*Painting.*) I'm starting on the hip now.

LULU: Corticelli must be really special.

SCHWARZ: She's one of the ones, that's all.

LULU: You know her?

SCHWARZ: God forbid. —She happens to have that great gift: to be able to fill the house with her presence—people a hundred yards away included—just by moving. Hence the gigantic salary. For one step that makes her skirt fly upwards she gets more money than I get for a picture I work on for nine months.

LULU: I feel—I don't know...

SCHWARZ: What's the matter? You're pale.

LULU: The first time he leaves me alone with a stranger...

SCHWARZ: But Dr. Goll has a practice.

LULU: But Lisa is always around.

SCHWARZ: Your housekeeper?

LULU: Where she came from I don't know. But she's run things for him for fifty years.

SCHWARZ: But you help out at times?

LULU: No. She puts me to bed at night and dresses me in the morning. She bathes me and does my hair and drinks absinthe all day.

SCHWARZ: God.

LULU: And when I sneak a drop of absinthe she boxes my ears.

SCHWARZ: Does your husband allow that?

LULU: He takes her part.

SCHWARZ: That you put up with such a life!

LULU: I read. French mostly.

SCHWARZ: You should throw the old bitch out on the street, you have a perfect right to.

LULU: And then?

SCHWARZ: Then? Why, then...

LULU: I am nothing without her. Who will dress me for my dance lesson?

SCHWARZ: You can dress yourself.

LULU: I don't know myself well enough.

SCHWARZ: What does she dress you in?

LULU: As little as possible.

SCHWARZ: God have mercy.

LULU: I'm not inventive.

SCHWARZ: Who gives you dance lessons?

LULU: He does. (SCHWARZ *almost drops his brush.*) Paint.

SCHWARZ: (*Who does.*)—I'd like to see him demonstrating those dances!

LULU: He knows all the dances: Czardas, Samaqueca, Negro Dances, Russian, Sailor Dances—

SCHWARZ: Don't you just die laughing?

LULU: He only tells me how. I dance alone. He plays the fiddle.

SCHWARZ: With you in costume?

LULU: I have two rooms full of costumes.

SCHWARZ: (*Drawing breath.*) The world is curiously constructed.

LULU: For which I must be grateful.

SCHWARZ: When do you dance?

LULU: After dinner.

SCHWARZ: Every evening?

LULU: Yes.

SCHWARZ: Tell me about it. It's easier to paint.

LULU: In winter we were in Paris. Every evening we'd see another dancer, and when we got home I was supposed to do as well as he or she did...It was frightful.

SCHWARZ: There must be much misery in Paris...

LULU: We went out by night only. All day long he was at the Medical School and I was home asleep, or sitting by the fire...

SCHWARZ: Then you saw little of the real Paris?

LULU: Toward the end of the day I took lessons from Eugenie Fougère, my legs were sore for six months after. She showed me costumes, she liked me—

SCHWARZ: How are your costumes?

LULU: In one, I'm a fisherman—boy, rather—and have to dance in heavy wooden shoes: shirt of coarse linen, open in front, short, broad sleeves, short, wide pants of coarse wool—

SCHWARZ: And the old man sits facing you?

LULU: Nothing shows.

SCHWARZ: Isn't it very repulsive?

LULU: Why?

SCHWARZ: Is that a marriage?

LULU: Every Thursday Dr. Schoning comes.

SCHWARZ: He didn't tell me he knew you.

LULU: Prince Polossov was there too. Then I was Eve...

SCHWARZ: I see.

LULU: High red boots, laced up—and violet socks—my hair in a knot, Greek style—with a red ribbon...

SCHWARZ: (*Sinking down.*) I can't go on.

LULU: Paint.

SCHWARZ: My arm is stiff.

LULU: It was never stiff before.

SCHWARZ: The light has changed too.

LULU: Which can be regulated by the curtains.

SCHWARZ: What I'm painting now, I would scratch out as soon as you left.

LULU: Makes no difference.

SCHWARZ: It's all reflections, not pure light now.

LULU: You've never taken breaks.

SCHWARZ: That's the problem. And it doesn't improve the painting. But the Dean of the Medical School, how can one make a man like that understand?

LULU: You only have to mention it to Dr. Schoning.

SCHWARZ: What can *he* do about it?

LULU: You never know.

SCHWARZ: I don't see how you put up with it.

LULU: Easy.

SCHWARZ: Just standing there as Pierrot, yes, as long as you don't freeze.

LULU: Oh, you should see me at home.

SCHWARZ: Your dance lesson?

LULU: All day, when he's working at home, I'm almost always in my chemise.

SCHWARZ: Just your chemise?

LULU: It's a warm house. And I'm used to it.

SCHWARZ: One learns something new every day!

LULU: I let my hair down and tie it in a bow. Yesterday I wore a dark green chemise with white bows.

SCHWARZ: Of coarse linen?

LULU: All silk. Long, light green stockings—and my white dance slippers. A pink bow in my hair—garters in quite tender pink...

SCHWARZ: Pure bordello style.

LULU: But cozy enough, especially in winter, when the Salon is nice and warm—you can breathe...

SCHWARZ: That you can do anyway.

LULU: In this Pierrot costume too...I feel good—

SCHWARZ: Really?

LULU: (*With an intake of breath.*) Well, you see...

SCHWARZ: Enough. Stop. (*He jumps up, throws brush and palette to one side, and walks excitedly up and down.*) The shoe-shine boy has only her feet to deal with, and shoe polish doesn't eat up all his money—If there was nothing to eat in the house, no woman in the world would pretend to be offering me oysters.

LULU: (*Imploring.*) Paint!

SCHWARZ: What drives the fellow to this rehearsal?

LULU: He won't stay much longer. —I *prefer* it when we're three.

SCHWARZ: (*Back at his easel, painting.*) Autumn leaves, autumn leaves!

LULU: I didn't make the costume myself. He designed it and the theater tailor cut it. —I didn't want to annoy you...

SCHWARZ: Strangulation of the soul. (*Lowers his brush.*) It's no good, it's no good.

LULU: Paint, *please.*

SCHWARZ: When the colors are dancing before my eyes?

LULU: Then *pretend* to be painting.

SCHWARZ: I see will o'the wisps.

LULU: He'll be right back. For your own sake, paint.

SCHWARZ: (*Beginning again.*) Of course. —As an artist, I can't afford to be accused of Immorality! And anyway it takes a Dean to afford such luxury.

LULU: (*Since he is painting now.*) Thank God.

SCHWARZ: The artist is a martyr to his profession. —If you'd hold the trousers a bit higher?

LULU: Even higher?

SCHWARZ: Just a bit.

LULU: That won't do. One sees my skin.

SCHWARZ: (*Stepping on the platform.*) Allow me.

LULU: It won't do.

SCHWARZ: Why not?

LULU: My stockings aren't long enough.

SCHWARZ: (*Taking her hand.*) I'll show you.

LULU: (*Throws the shepherd's crook in his face.*) Leave me alone. (*She hurries to the entrance.*)

SCHWARZ: (*Following.*) Where are you going?

LULU: You can't have me yet.

SCHWARZ: You don't understand a joke. (*He urges her into a corner, left.*)

LULU: (*Fleeing, right.*) I understand jokes, I understand the whole thing. —Let me go. You'll get nowhere with me by force!

SCHWARZ: (*Stepping back.*) Please!

LULU: (*Returning to the platform.*) Get back to work. —You have
no right to bother me.

SCHWARZ: (*Approaching her.*) Hold that position...

LULU: First get behind your easel. (*She flees behind the ottoman
since* SCHWARZ *tries to grab her.*)

SCHWARZ: (*Right of ottoman.*) As soon as I've punished you.

LULU: (*At the lower end.*) First you must catch me.

SCHWARZ: (*Tries to catch her from the left.*) Watch me do it.

LULU: (*Retreating, right.*) What do you know? Watch me do it.
(*She teases him now.*) Tra la la.

SCHWARZ: As I hope to be saved...(*Groping his way around the
ottoman, right.*)

LULU: (*Retreating, left.*) Boom, boom!

SCHWARZ: (*At the upper end.*) You'll pay for this.

LULU: (*Opposite, rising.*) Get back to work. —You won't catch
me, I promise you.

SCHWARZ: (*Jerking himself now left, now right.*) Just a moment.

LULU: (*Ditto.*) In long skirts I maybe couldn't defend myself...

SCHWARZ: Don't be childish.

LULU:...but as Pierrot...

SCHWARZ: Just you wait.

LULU: I only have a chemise on underneath.

SCHWARZ: (*Throws himself diagonally across the ottoman.*) Gotcha!

LULU: (*Throwing the tiger's skin over his head.*) So there! (*She
jumps across the platform and clambers up the ladder.*) I'm the
sun—I shine—I emit beams of brilliant light—I can see all
the cities of Germany!

SCHWARZ: (*Unwrapping himself.*) Tiger skin!

LULU: (*Holding on to the ladder with her left hand, her right arm
upright.*) I reach for the clouds! I stick stars in my hair!

SCHWARZ: (*Climbing up after her.*) And I'll shake this thing till
you fall!

LULU: (*Climbing higher.*) And if you don't stop, I'll push the
ladder over.

SCHWARZ: You're so beautiful.

LULU: I'll kick your head in.

SCHWARZ: I see sheet lightning.

LULU: Keep your claws off my legs!

SCHWARZ: Stop wriggling or I'll drag you down.

LULU: God save Poland!* (*She pushes the ladder over. She is now down on the platform throwing the Spanish screen over* SCHWARZ's *head. He had picked himself up but is groaning. Hurrying forward.*) Up boys, and at'em! God is on our side! (*Right, near the easels, following* SCHWARZ's *movements.*) I told you, you wouldn't get me.

SCHWARZ: (*Creeping forward.*) Just keep away from the pictures!

LULU: Me and my wolf pack, we're on our way out of here!

SCHWARZ: (*Coming forward.*) If you can just...(*He tries to take hold.*)

LULU: Keep away from me or...(*Since* SCHWARZ *is still reaching for her.*)..this is what I do. (*She takes the easel with the pastel portrait and throws it at him. Picture and frame hit the floor with a crash.*)

SCHWARZ: Merciful heaven!

LULU: (*Back, right.*) Any damage is your own doing.

SCHWARZ: The rent for this studio! —My trip! My trip to Norway!

LULU: Then why chase me around?

SCHWARZ: Wha'do I care now? (*He storms after her.*)

LULU: (*Leaps over the ottoman and the overturned ladder and, coming to the front of the platform, turns a somersault on the carpet.*) A trench—don't fall into it! (*But having jumped up, her foot goes through the picture frame and she falls.*)

SCHWARZ: (*Falls on her now.*) Got you.

LULU: (*Managing to wriggle out of his grip.*) You're squeezing me.

SCHWARZ: (*Gets up and follows her.*)

LULU: (*At back.*) Leave me in peace now—I feel sick—

* Wedekind probably intended Lulu to sing the opening phrase of a Polish Hymn that dates back to 1796.

SCHWARZ: (*Stumbling over the Spanish screen.*) I'll show no mercy now.

LULU: (*Out of breath, coming forward.*) I feel...oh...I feel...oh, my God! (*She sinks down on the ottoman.*)

SCHWARZ: (*Gasping desperately for breath.*) O God...Who madest Woman! (*He goes to the back and bolts the door. Returning.*) This world is a mean sort of place...makes me think of a salver, a huge tray—(*He places himself next to her.*)

LULU: (*Opening her eyes.*) I fell down.

SCHWARZ: The world is mean.

LULU: Deep down.

SCHWARZ: How're you doing?

LULU: Stormy weather.

SCHWARZ: (*Kisses her bare arm.*) Get undressed.

LULU: It's too cold.

SCHWARZ: Please! (*He tries to take her costume off.*)

LULU: Stop it.

SCHWARZ: Then come...

LULU: Come where?

SCHWARZ: Into the bedroom.

LULU: He may be back.

SCHWARZ: Just for a minute.

LULU: What for?

SCHWARZ: I love you.

LULU: (*Shuddering.*) Oh...

SCHWARZ: (*Taking her pants off.*) My sweet...

LULU: (*Holding his hand back.*) Stop it.

SCHWARZ: (*Kissing her.*) Then come.

LULU: Here is better.

SCHWARZ: Here?

LULU: If you want to.

SCHWARZ: Then let me undress you.

LULU: What for?

SCHWARZ: Because I love you.

LULU: I am yours.
SCHWARZ: Oh, please.
LULU: I am yours.
SCHWARZ: O my God!
LULU: If you want to.
SCHWARZ: You are cruel.
LULU: So why don't you...?
SCHWARZ: Please, dear girl...
LULU: I am yours.
SCHWARZ: Be nice to me.
LULU: I am being nice to you.
SCHWARZ: Then get undressed.
LULU: What for?
SCHWARZ: That Pierrot costume...
LULU: But I am yours.
SCHWARZ: Nelly...
LULU: How'd you mean, my Pierrot...?
SCHWARZ: Nelly...Nelly...
LULU: But I'm not Nelly.
SCHWARZ: Your Pierrot costume...
LULU: My name is Lulu.
SCHWARZ: I would call you Eve.
LULU: As you wish.
SCHWARZ: Then be nice to me.
LULU: As you wish.
SCHWARZ: Eve.
LULU: What do you want me to do?
SCHWARZ: Get undressed.
LULU: What for?
SCHWARZ: You're toying with me.
LULU: You don't want to?
SCHWARZ: I don't want...?
LULU: I am yours.
SCHWARZ: But, dear Eve...

LULU: And why not?

SCHWARZ: Please!

LULU: You don't like me.

SCHWARZ: Merciful God!

LULU: Come...

SCHWARZ: Eve! Eve!

LULU: All right, then don't.

SCHWARZ: You...(*He jumps up, bewildered, out of control.*) My God...God, God, God...God in Heaven!

LULU: (*An outcry.*) Don't do me in, don't!

SCHWARZ: Anything can happen.

LULU: (*Sitting up, almost.*) I don't believe you've ever made love.

SCHWARZ: (*Quickly turning to face her, blushing to the roots of his hair.*) But you haven't either.

LULU: Me?

SCHWARZ: How old are you?

LULU: Eighteen. And you?

SCHWARZ: Twenty-eight—it sounds crazy, crazy, I know, it sounds insane, but it can happen!

GOLL: (*Outside.*) Open the door!

LULU: (*Jumping up.*) Hide me. My God! You must hide me.

GOLL: (*Beating on the door.*) Open up!

SCHWARZ: Merciful heaven! (*Makes for the door.*)

LULU: (*Holds him back.*) You will not!

GOLL: (*Beating on the door.*) Open up!

LULU: (*Has sunk down before* SCHWARZ *and is embracing his knees.*) He'll beat me to death. Hide me!

SCHWARZ: Where? Where? (*The door falls in with a crash.*)

SCENE FIVE. Goll. The foregoing.

GOLL: (*Dark red, with bloodshot eyes, falls on* SCHWARZ *with raised stick.*)—You dog—you dogs, you—(*He tumbles head first on to the floorboards.*)

SCHWARZ: (*Stands there trembling, with sagging knees.*)

LULU: (*Has fled to the door. Pause.*)

SCHWARZ: (*Approaching* GOLL'*s body.*) Herr—Herr Doktor!

LULU (*In the doorway.*) First tidy up the studio.

SCHWARZ: Quiet!

(*Pause.*)

LULU: (*Daring to come forward.*) He is not...

SCHWARZ: (*Raises* GOLL'*s head.*) Herr Doktor. (*Stepping back.*) He's bleeding.

LULU: Must've given himself a bloody nose.

SCHWARZ: Help me get him on to the ottoman.

LULU: (*Stepping back.*) No...No...

SCHWARZ: (*Tries to turn the body round.*) Herr Doktor, Herr Doktor...

LULU: (*Motionless.*) He evaded the issue.

SCHWARZ: A stroke. It could be a stroke. Help me a bit.

LULU: Even together we can't lift him.

SCHWARZ: (*Straightening up.*) This can be quite a scene.

LULU: He is frightfully heavy.

SCHWARZ: We must send for a doctor. (*Taking* GOLL'*s hat.*) Do me a favor and tidy up the frames and things. (*Leaving.*) I can tear up the other picture now...

SCENE SIX. Lulu. Goll.

LULU: (*Not yet close to* GOLL.) All of a sudden, he'll jump up! (*In a whisper.*) Hugs and kisses! (*Both hands to her temples.*) He takes no notice. (*Walking round him but giving him a wide berth.*) His pants are all torn but it doesn't bother him. (*She is behind him now.*) Hugging, kissing...(*She touches him with the point of her shoe.*) Piglet! (*Drawing back.*) He means it. (*She stares into space.*) He'll never make me do tricks again. (*Lost in thought she walks, right.*) He's through with me, what do I do now? Clothes I have. (*Turning to face the bedroom.*) I don't know how to dress, only how to *un*dress. (*She comes forward and bends over the body.*) Such a strange wild face—if he were to get up now—(*Getting up.*) And no one here to close his eyes—

SCENE SEVEN. Schwarz. The foregoing.

SCHWARZ: (*Entering quickly.*) Still not conscious?

LULU: (*Comes forward, left.*) What am I gonna do?

SCHWARZ: (*Bending over* GOLL.) Herr Doktor!

LULU: I don't think he's going to come to.

SCHWARZ: Herr Doktor!

LULU: He's kinda lost the thread.

SCHWARZ: Have some decency.

LULU: He never ventured to dream that...

SCHWARZ: (*Trying to raise the body.*) He weighs three hundred pounds.

LULU: And going cold without realizing.

SCHWARZ: (*Turning* GOLL *on his back.*) Herr Doktor! Herr...(*Pointing out a cushion to* LULU.) Give me that cushion.

LULU: (*Handing him the cushion.*) If I danced the Samaqueca* for him...

SCHWARZ: (*Pushing the cushion under* GOLL*'s head.*) The doctor will be here any minute.

LULU: But for that I'd have to be alone with him.

SCHWARZ:...I've sent the housekeeper to fetch him.

LULU: He never responded to medication of any kind.

SCHWARZ: One does what one can.

LULU: He put no stock in that stuff.

SCHWARZ: You might at least change your clothes.

---

* A South American dance that Wedekind had learned from his mother. In it, a girl stands in the middle, and the boy dances around her. Obviously, the arrangement is reversed when Lulu dances around her man.

LULU: If only there was someone to help me.

SCHWARZ: For God's sake, do it yourself.

LULU: I don't know how.

SCHWARZ: Then *I* could...

LULU: But first close his eyes.

SCHWARZ: My God, do you really think...

LULU: Hm.

SCHWARZ: I don't know.

LULU: Then if not...

SCHWARZ: I've never seen anyone die.

LULU: Then don't worry about it.

SCHWARZ: You are a horror.

LULU: And you?

SCHWARZ: (*Looks at her wide eyed.*)

LULU: I'll have to face the music, too.

SCHWARZ: At least keep your trap shut.

LULU: You too.

SCHWARZ: I don't need telling.

LULU: Now do it.

SCHWARZ: What?

LULU: Or it will be too late.

SCHWARZ: That would be your affair.

LULU: My affair?

SCHWARZ: How about me?

LULU: He stares me right in the face.

SCHWARZ: He stares ME right in the face.

LULU: Call yourself a man?

SCHWARZ: (*Closing* GOLL's *eyes.*) It's the first time I ever—

LULU: You didn't do it for your parents?

SCHWARZ: No.

LULU: You'd left home?

SCHWARZ: No.

LULU: You were scared?

SCHWARZ: (*Violently.*) No!

LULU: (*Shrinking back.*) I didn't mean to insult you.

SCHWARZ: My parents are still alive.

LULU: Then you have someone.

SCHWARZ: No, no, they're poor as mice.

LULU: So was I.

SCHWARZ: You?

LULU: I'm rich *now*.

SCHWARZ: (*Looks at her and shakes his head.*) You give me the creeps. (*Excited, he walks up and down, to himself.*) It's not her fault.

LULU: (*To herself.*) What I do...(*Long pause.* LULU *stands motionless, her gaze on* GOLL. SCHWARZ *looks at her from the side.*)

SCHWARZ: (*Taking both her hands in his.*) Look me in the eye.

LULU: What d'you want?

SCHWARZ: Look at me.

LULU: What do you want to see?

SCHWARZ: Your eyes. (*He steers her to the ottoman and makes her sit beside him.*) Look in *my* eyes.

LULU: (*Doing so.*) I see myself there—as Pierrot.

SCHWARZ: (*Jumping up, pushing her away.*) The devil. The devil is in this.

LULU: I must get changed.

SCHWARZ: (*Holding her back.*) One question. Just one—

LULU: I can't answer it.

SCHWARZ: (*Drawing her back to the ottoman.*) Can you—can you...?

LULU: Yes?

SCHWARZ: What? Tell the truth?

LULU: I don't know.

SCHWARZ: You must be able to tell the truth?

LULU: I don't know.

SCHWARZ: Do you believe in a Creator?*

---

* This is a question that Goethe's Gretchen puts to Faust. The series of "I don't know"'s echoes the responses of the eponymous hero in Act One of Wagner's Parsifal.

LULU: I don't know. Leave me alone. You're nuts.

SCHWARZ: (*Holding her back.*) Can you swear by all that's sacred?

LULU: I don't know.

SCHWARZ: What DO you believe in?

LULU: I don't know.

SCHWARZ: Is there a soul in your body?

LULU: I don't know.

SCHWARZ: Are you still a virgin?

(*Pause.*)

LULU: I don't know.

SCHWARZ: God in Heaven! (*He gets up and walks left, wringing his hands.*)

LULU: (*Without moving.*) I don't know.

SCHWARZ: (*Looking at* GOLL.) *He* knows.

LULU: (*Approaching him.*) Anything else you wanna know?

SCHWARZ: I want to know everything!

LULU: Since I got married—every night that God let happen, I had to dance, half naked...

SCHWARZ: I don't want to hear it, it tells me nothing!

LULU: In any case why *shouldn't* I...

SCHWARZ: What??

LULU: YOU can...

SCHWARZ: Have you no shame?!

LULU: It was you that asked.

SCHWARZ: Go and get dressed.

SCENE EIGHT. Schwarz. Goll. Later Lulu.

SCHWARZ: (*Looking in the direction of* GOLL.) What can she do about it? —I could raise her above it all. Awake the soul within her. She'd go right along with that. A lost person...My parents, my poor parents...I'm poor...yet so lucky now too...Do I love her? Does she love me, she me? — She loves me, so she says. —I love her. —She loves me. —

Loves me. My first go at marriage...I feel so miserable—I'd like to change places with you, yeah, with you, stand up, old man, I'll give her back to you, your doll, your puppet, I'll give you my youth for the purpose. I lack the guts to live. To love. You can begin again with my strengths, my unbroken strengths, and make up for—you can—He's opening his mouth—Mouth open and eyes closed—like kids—I'm not a kid—I was never a kid—(*Sighing.*) What I am (*Kneeling he ties a handkerchief around* GOLL's *head.*) is an old maid. I'm asking Heaven, yes, Heaven, I'm praying now: make me capable of happiness, give me the courage for it, the courage, the power, and the glory—a little bit of happiness—for her sake—

LULU: (*Opens the bedroom door.*) Now, if you would be so kind...

END OF ACT ONE

LULU has married Edward SCHWARZ, painter.

ACT TWO

Small, very elegant drawing room. Back left, main entrance. Left and right, side doors. On the back wall over the fireplace in a splendid brocade frame, the picture of Lulu as Pierrot. Downstage right, several armchairs around a small Chinese table. Numerous pictures in charming gold frames, some of them unfinished. Right, a desk in carved ebony.

SCENE ONE. Schwarz. Lulu.

Down right, schwarzin an easy chair, lulu on his knee in a Nile-green silk night dress with fichu collar abundantly décolleté.

LULU: (*Pulling free from his importunate advances.*)—In broad daylight...

SCHWARZ: (*Embracing her.*) But you are mine...

LULU: You are dreadful...

SCHWARZ: What can I do about it?

LULU: You're killing me...

SCHWARZ: It's all your fault...

LULU: (*Burying her face in his bosom.*) Just wait a while...

SCHWARZ: Till winter comes?

LULU: Till evening, just.

SCHWARZ: It's getting to be evening.

LULU: Till I have you to myself.

SCHWARZ: What more is needed than...

LULU: You ...you...

SCHWARZ: This *is* me.

LULU: Till we're free.

SCHWARZ: Surely that's all one?

LULU: No...

SCHWARZ: Oh, please...

LULU: Like children...

SCHWARZ: Like children...

LULU: It's sinful...

SCHWARZ: Let's be sinful...

LULU: You can do it by yourself...

SCHWARZ: Never. I never did *that*. (*He tries to pull her skirt up.*)

LULU: (*Holds her dress so tight under her knees that her dark green slippers fall off her feet.*) I'm telling you...

SCHWARZ: You're not being nice...

LULU: (*Kissing him.*) You're all the sweeter to...

SCHWARZ: I'm all too sweet...

LULU: Not by a long shot.

SCHWARZ: So say you.

LULU: You know I'm right.

SCHWARZ: I only have to hear you walk along...

LULU: (*Kissing him.*) Beloved!

SCHWARZ: And discretion is thrown to the winds!

LULU: I'll have to go barefoot...

SCHWARZ: That's all we need.

LULU: Would I deliberately destroy you?

SCHWARZ: Death would be welcome...

LULU: (*Kissing him.*) But where would it leave *me*?

SCHWARZ: (*Shaking himself.*) Oh...Eve...

LULU: Wait I've something to tell you...

SCHWARZ: From today's newspaper?

LULU: A surprise...

SCHWARZ: Surprises faze me. The world could come to an end. In the morning I fear that by evening you may be bitten by a mad dog. Today I live in dread that revolution may break out tomorrow. Tomorrow I'll be dreading an insect bite or who knows what that might end our happiness.

LULU: (*Sinking on his chest, whispers in his ear.*)

SCHWARZ: Not possible...!

LULU: (*Rising with a smile.*) It is...

SCHWARZ: You're a mother?

LULU: Not yet.

SCHWARZ: (*Embracing her passionately.*) Eve! Eve! MY Eve—

LULU: Of course I'd have enjoyed being in love and free a while longer...

SCHWARZ: No, no. You're making me so happy!

LULU: (*Covering her face.*) D'you have a heart?

SCHWARZ: I do, I do.

LULU: I'd have waited happily...

SCHWARZ: (*Stroking her.*) Thank you, *from* my heart, a thousand thank yous!

LULU: (*Picking herself up.*) It's your doing...

SCHWARZ: Yours! Yours ten times more!

LULU: Well, let's not quarrel about it...

SCHWARZ: What all have you managed to do!?

LULU: What's done is done.

SCHWARZ: Are you sure of it?

LULU: (*Nodding.*) For the last two weeks.

SCHWARZ: How could you keep quiet so long?

LULU: So often I was in tears half the night.

SCHWARZ: The only blessing, the only one, that was lacking...Our life was just heaven already.

LULU: I tried everything.

SCHWARZ: You rascal. —I can face it, your...confinement and so on...I'm not afraid. I certainly can take care of more than two people, so just keep it up, my dear...I've built up a terrific reputation. The art dealers can't wait for me to come up with another picture. And why have I brought things this far? What was I working towards if not—my family?

LULU: I wouldn't claim—

SCHWARZ: Ever since I've had *you*, I've been blessed by God, I've known what I am, and got recognition for it. I've you to thank for my self confidence, my pride as an artist, my joy in creating art. You are my happiness, you've *built up* my business, brick by brick. It's the way you are: you bloom, you fade for me! Me! Your body lives for me! Yes, I had to fish you out! I was man enough and now my cup runneth over, my reputation grows by leaps and bounds, and you'll add a jewel to my crown with every year that passes.

LULU: (*Interrupting.*) Could we take a short walk out in the open?

SCHWARZ: I must get back to my work. There's a model waiting for me. (*He picks up paintbrush and palette off the floor. Kissing* LULU.) Till...till this evening...I'll be painting my—

LULU: I'm afraid.

SCHWARZ: My Iphigenia.* She still isn't *there*....still isn't an expression of the *me* you'll see in her, oh , by the end of the March. —Then there are the five commissions from the United States.

LULU: (*Rocking herself on his knee.*) Are you mad at me?

SCHWARZ: (*Puts brush and palette on one side again.*) I'm an artist, that's my excuse, if I've got one. Then too, you are frightfully...turbulent...

LULU: (*Shudders.*)

SCHWARZ: You are, you are.

LULU: I feel a little unhinged.

SCHWARZ: I'm not surprised.

LULU: Well may you laugh.

SCHWARZ: Don't blame me.

LULU: Who else?

SCHWARZ: It's your beauty.

LULU: (*Alluding to the childbirth.*) I'm going to get hurt.

SCHWARZ: You're so sweet!

LULU: You are inhuman.

SCHWARZ: How can I help it?

LULU: I can't be other than female.

SCHWARZ: You're female all right.

LULU: And I wish I was an *ugly* female.

* The Iphigenia the German reader would think of is Goethe's 18th-century classical version—a neat contrast to Alva's Superwoman.

SCHWARZ: God forbid!

LULU: For a short while...three weeks...

SCHWARZ: A misfortune...

LULU: To think of being a child again knowing nothing—to be glad about something, glad about growing up. To be able to laugh again—how great that would be—to be once again, somewhat, a virgin.

SCHWARZ: (*Stroking her hair.*) Almighty God!

LULU: I'd like to play in the street again.

SCHWARZ: The world is brutal, yes, it's a brutal world, and your destiny, surely, is sacrifice...a sort of death sentence—a blessed death, of course...surrender to it...

LULU: I cry out sometimes.

SCHWARZ: I've often noticed that. —I don't know what makes me so fearful.

LULU: I wouldn't wish anyone...

SCHWARZ: It's not just your flesh...

LULU: My poor flesh...

SCHWARZ: I've given it a lot of thought.

LULU:...it's like meat that's well done.

SCHWARZ: Oh, one get's accustomed...

LULU: I don't know if I'm lying on silk sheets or bare floorboards.

SCHWARZ: (*Lost in thought.*) And it's not your style to toss and turn...even though you do it quite divinely...

LULU: My skin was so tender. If I ran the tips of my finger over my knees, it'd make pink stripes across the skin.

SCHWARZ: I had such suspicions about your kisses.

LULU: Maybe my underwear...

SCHWARZ: God forbid.

LULU: I won't wear any in future!

SCHWARZ: But it's not your kisses!

LULU: (*Kissing him.*) No?

SCHWARZ: You're so stingy with them.

LULU: (*Kissing him.*) With my kisses?

SCHWARZ: Where did you learn this?

LULU: Before I came into this world...

SCHWARZ: Little goose!

LULU: From Mammakins.

SCHWARZ: I see.

LULU: One person can.

SCHWARZ: I take your word for it.

LULU: Another cannot.

SCHWARZ: I'd never have guessed.

LULU: *You* can.

SCHWARZ: So what does it depend on?

LULU: ...without kisses...

SCHWARZ: Tell me the secret.

LULU: It makes no difference.

SCHWARZ: A riddle. —I need only bring you before my mind's eye...

LULU: (*Kissing him.*) Poor boy.

SCHWARZ: ...And I see your beauty, your arms and legs, your torso...(*He raises her skirt so that her bright green stockings are seen above the knee.*)—There's no sensuality in the lines of your legs...

LULU: (*Demurring.*)—Just a minute ago we were in bed together!

SCHWARZ: (*Lost in his soulful gazing upon knees.*) They are too spiritual...too chaste.

LULU: (*Covering her knees.*) Why rack your brains about—?

SCHWARZ: It must be something...

LULU: (*Kissing him.*) Quiet...

SCHWARZ: A matter of...

LULU: (*Closing his mouth.*) No! —No!

SCHWARZ: A matter of...

LULU: (*Showers him with kisses.*) Da-da-da-da-da...

SCHWARZ: You well know...

LULU: (*Straightening up, crossing her feet.*) At that I have no power over it and can't change it.

SCHWARZ: (*Pressing her to him.*) I won't let you change it, my child, you won't be allowed to change it, it's your soul, your all in all.

LULU: (*Sinking back.*) You drive me crazy. (*Closing her eyes, opening her lips.*) I'm so hot, so...

SCHWARZ: (*Lifts her gently up and lays her back in the easy chair.*) Henrietta is out doing the shopping...

LULU: (*Hands between knees.*) Turn the key.

SCHWARZ: (*Goes to the back and locks the door. But now there's a ring in the corridor.*) Hang whoever it is!

LULU: We're not at home.

SCHWARZ: It may be the art dealer.

LULU: I don't care if it's the Kaiser!

SCHWARZ: One moment. (*He goes out.*)

SCENE TWO. Lulu.

LULU: (*Alone, motionless, stares into space.*) You—you—you here? Oh, oh, all right then.

SCENE THREE. Lulu. Schwarz.

SCHWARZ: (*Coming back.*) A beggar. Says he fought in the war. —Give me fifty pfennigs, I have no cash on me. (*He bends down to kiss her.*)

LULU: Now go—

SCHWARZ: (*Brush and palette in hand again.*) Yes. Time for me to get back to Iphigenia! I kept the model waiting all the time you and I were fooling around! (*As he leaves.*) Give him fifty pfennigs. (*He leaves, on the right.*)

LULU: (*Rises, slowly, sets her clothes straight, pulls her hair back, and goes to the door.*)

SCENE FOUR. Lulu. Schigolch.

SCHIGOLCH: (*Brought in by* LULU.)—I'd picked someone huskier, broader in the chest. He's nervous. Sagged a bit at the knees when he caught sight of me.

LULU: (*Placing a chair for him.*) Why d'you have to *beg* from him?

SCHIGOLCH: Why else lug my carcass over here? It's troublesome coming over in this heat. You told me he worked mornings with his coloring brush?

LULU: Today he didn't. —How much d'you want?

SCHIGOLCH: Only two hundred—if you have it—three hundred would also do. My two best customers have gone away without a word.

LULU: (*Goes to the desk on the right and rummages in the drawer.*) Am I tired!

SCHIGOLCH: (*Looking around the room.*) Pretty much as I imagined it. I've been wanting to see how you made out.

LULU: Well?

SCHIGOLCH: I'm overwhelmed. (*Looking upwards.*) Like my place fifty years ago. —None of this Chinesey stuff back then, no, it was rusty old swords for us! —Hell, you've been going some. (*While scraping the rug.*) These carpets...!

LULU: (*Gives him three bank notes.*) I go barefoot when no one's around.

SCHIGOLCH: (*Noting her picture.*) This is you?

LULU: Elegant?

SCHIGOLCH: If it's all the real thing.

LULU: Sumpn sweet to drink?

SCHIGOLCH: Like what?

LULU: (*Getting up.*) "Elixir of Life." Product of Belgium.

SCHIGOLCH: Belgium or East Africa, that stuff's just camomile tea to me. Does he drink?

LULU: I've been doing without that. —(*Coming down front.*)

Spirituous fluids have varied effects.

SCHIGOLCH: He breaks out?

LULU: (*Filling the glasses.*) He falls asleep.

SCHIGOLCH: When he's drunk, you can see into his guts.

LULU: I'd rather not. (*Sits opposite* SCHIGOLCH.) Tell me your story.

SCHIGOLCH: The roads get longer, a guy's legs grow shorter.

LULU: And your harmonica?

SCHIGOLCH: Doesn't breathe right. Like me with my asthma. But like I always say, a repair job ain't worth the trouble any more. (*They clink glasses.*)

LULU: (*Emptying her glass.*) I thought you were finished, earlier.

SCHIGOLCH: I thought so too. —But the sun goes down, and you still can't get to sleep. I'm looking forward to the winter when my—my—my (*Coughing.*)—dear old asthma can hope to find transportation facilities.

LULU: (*Filling the glasses.*) You think we might all have forgotten you?

SCHIGOLCH: You might. Things weren't going according to plan. (*Stroking her knees.*) Now *you* talk...it's been so long...my little Lulu.

LULU: (*Pulling back from him, smiling.*) Life passes comprehension.

SCHIGOLCH: You're still so young.

LULU: To think you call me Lulu.

SCHIGOLCH: Did I ever call you anything else?

LULU: I haven't been called Lulu in human memory.

SCHIGOLCH: They call you something else?

LULU: Lulu sounds—antedeluvian.

SCHIGOLCH: Well, whadda ya know?

LULU: I'm now called...

SCHIGOLCH: As if it wasn't the same old honey pot!

LULU: You think...?

SCHIGOLCH: So what's it now?

LULU: Eve.

SCHIGOLCH: Six of one, half a dozen of the other.

LULU: Not bad: Eve.

SCHIGOLCH: (*Looks around.*) It's what I dreamed of for you. It's just right for you. —And what may that be?

LULU: (*Spraying herself from a perfume bottle.*) Heliotrope.

SCHIGOLCH: Does it smell better than you?

LULU: When I think...

SCHIGOLCH: (*Stroking her knees.*) How are you doing? —Do you keep up with your French?

LULU: I go to bed and sleep.

SCHIGOLCH: That's *noble*. It always looks good. What else?

LULU: I stretch out. 'Till something clicks.

SCHIGOLCH: And when it *has* clicked?

LULU: Why does all this interest you?

SCHIGOLCH: Why, oh why? —I'd rather live 'till the last trumpet sounds and forego the pleasures of heaven than know my Lulu here below to be tangled in troubles—Why does it interest me? —It's my sympathy for you, my capacity for higher things—things divine, so to speak. But I still have an understanding of this world below.

LULU: I don't.

SCHIGOLCH: Because you're doing too good.

LULU: 'Till it drives me silly.

SCHIGOLCH: Doing better than with the old dancing bear?

LULU: I don't dance any more.

SCHIGOLCH: The time came to turn him into money?

LULU: And now I'm...

SCHIGOLCH: Speak, let your heart speak, my child. I had confidence in you when you were nothing but two big eyes with a big mouth under them.

LULU: I'm an animal.

SCHIGOLCH: But what an animal!

LULU: I know—I'm elegant.

SCHIGOLCH: An elegant animal. A thing of splendor.

LULU: You were the animal *trainer*.

SCHIGOLCH: Oh yes. —And now I can get myself buried. — We're through with our prejudices.

LULU: You were always through with prejudices.

SCHIGOLCH: Including prejudice against the woman who will wash my corpse.

LULU: You needn't fear being washed one last time.

SCHIGOLCH: Only to be dirty again after that!

LULU: (*Spraying him.*) Which would call you back to life again.

SCHIGOLCH: Not dirty: moldy.

LULU: Hold on a minute! Every evening I cover my whole body with scrag fat from the neck of a steer. With powder on top of that, I look like a marble statue. —It makes your skin like satin.

SCHIGOLCH: And worth all the trouble—on account of the fancy boy friend.

LULU: When the sheet is pulled back at night, I'm a peeled apple.

SCHIGOLCH: And no less a piece of dirt for all that.

LULU: No less. —I don't feel right unless I'm fit for biting all over.

SCHIGOLCH: Me too. Fit to bite. Fit to bite all over. —Give a big dinner soon. Open table.

LULU: The worms won't be getting many big dinners out of *you.*

SCHIGOLCH: Will your admirers preserve your body in alcohol? You're Helen of Troy only so long as you can move your arms and legs. After which? They won't even accept you at the zoo: the animals would belch. (*Rising.*) You might make good manure.

LULU: (*Rising.*) Have you quite finished?

SCHIGOLCH: Add this: on my grave, plant a turpentine tree.

LULU: I'll arrange for that.

SCHIGOLCH: I'll bet. —I dragged you naked out of a rathole.

LULU: You lifted me up with one hand and, with the other, used your suspenders to beat my behind. I didn't forget.

SCHIGOLCH: And it was called for. —(*He holds out his cheek.*) Bye now...

LULU: (*Kissing the cheek.*) Bye. (*She takes him out and brings* DR. SCHONING *in.*)

SCENE FIVE. Dr. Schoning. Lulu.

SCHONING: What's your father doing here, Mrs. Schwarz?

LULU: My father? —And how come I'm Mrs. Schwarz?

SCHONING: (*Uncertainly.*) I have to...speak with you...it'll take just a moment, Mrs. Schwarz.

LULU: With *me*? Why didn't you say so yesterday, DR. SCHONING?

SCHONING: (*Sitting.*) If I were Edward Schwarz, this character would never cross my threshold.

LULU: (*Settling into a chair.*) Well, for heaven's sake, what *do* you have in mind when...

SCHONING: Hear me out, Mrs. Schwarz.

LULU: Mrs. Schwarz!? —*He's* in his studio...

SCHONING: I tried to tell you yesterday, I tried to...

LULU: He's in his studio.

SCHONING: Please don't get so excited...

LULU: But you...it gives me the creeps...

SCHONING: Well, um, I want to ask that your visits to my place...

LULU: Visits?!

SCHONING: (*Getting it out.*) I wish to request that your visits to my place be discontinued.

LULU: You're out of your mind.

SCHONING: I'm requesting that your visits be discontinued.

LULU: What's come over you?

SCHONING: Did you understand what I said?

LULU: No.

SCHONING: I've been thinking it over for months. With your

interests at heart. It was always you and your happiness...

LULU: Want some "Elixir of Life", Product of Belgium?

SCHONING: Not now. —I want you to promise me...

LULU: What's happened to you? Since yesterday?

SCHONING: Nothing.

LULU: You're playing some game...

SCHONING: I have made a request. Twice.

LULU: You've caught a cold, maybe...

SCHONING: I'm quite well, thanks.

LULU: Me too.

SCHONING: If you won't listen...

LULU: I'm listening.

SCHONING: If you don't listen, you simply won't be allowed in, you will compel me to...

(LULU *gets up and walks up and down.*)

SCHONING: For my part, I shall leave no stone unturned to maintain your proper position in society. You can be just as proud of it as you were of...intimacy with me. —But they're not going to make a showpiece of me any more.

LULU: Don't toy with me. What have I done?

SCHONING: I pay a higher price than you do.

(*Pause.*)

LULU: (*Settling gracefully into a chair beside him, a hand on the arm.*) You want to—get married...

SCHONING: That too.

LULU: A union, not of the senses merely? To a higher being?

SCHONING: Will you be quiet?

LULU: As you wish.

SCHONING: I just don't want to fall between two stools.

LULU: May I ask...?

SCHONING: Fräulein zum Bergen.

LULU: (*Nods.*)

SCHONING: And nothing can be changed.

LULU: Do you know her?

SCHONING: I sat her on my knee, as a little girl.

LULU: Pretty?

SCHONING: Oh, she has claims.

LULU: She still doesn't know what's coming?

SCHONING: She's being filled in.

LULU: She's still in the rooming house?

SCHONING: From which she'll come straight to me.

LULU: Poor kid.

SCHONING: We visited her last week—her father and I. —One can't say too much in advance.

LULU: Is she sixteen yet?

SCHONING: She'll be everything she should be.

LULU: And the Baroness?

SCHONING: Has given the agonized, motherly nod.

LULU: How clever you are!

SCHONING: An act of gratitude.

LULU: I know. You saved her dear Papa from a jail sentence.

SCHONING: His hand in the cookie jar. The cookie jar belonged to the Order of...

LULU: So then you took on the Mama?

SCHONING: Which was only polite.

LULU: Yes. You...

SCHONING: As sure as there's a God in heaven!

LULU: I hope I look that good when *I'm* thirty-seven.

SCHONING: She's brought six children into the world.

LULU: No one would guess.

SCHONING: You don't see it in her, do you?

LULU: So she wanted to reward you...

SCHONING: Without, of course, embarrassing her husband. We only saw each other once. And I asked her to tell him everything.

LULU: You already had your eye on the daughter?

SCHONING: That too.

LULU: I won't add to her unhappiness: I'll never set foot in your house again.

SCHONING: Your word of...?

LULU: We can meet wherever else you want.

SCHONING: That will be nowhere. Ever. Except in the presence of your husband.

LULU: That's asking *too* much.

SCHONING: When he married you, your husband became my friend.

LULU: Mine too.

SCHONING: For you to go behind his back would be...unpleasant for me...

LULU: Dear God!

SCHONING: I've got used to him. At my age, one doesn't easily form attachments. —Now *he's* the only person who is closer to me than even...

LULU: Oh, you'll find friends enough when you remarry..

SCHONING: Thank you.

LULU: Wait a moment.

SCHONING: That's why I want no trouble with Schwarz.

LULU: There's no danger.

SCHONING: There is. He's such a child...

LULU: Such a dolt...

SCHONING: Or he'd have been on to you long ago.

LULU: It wouldn't have hurt any if he had been "on" to me. —He wouldn't have made himself ridiculous. He could have respected himself...

SCHONING: Why did you marry him?

LULU: I had yet to meet such an idiot.

SCHONING: Poor guy!

LULU: He thinks he's fortunate!

SCHONING: If his eyes should ever be opened!

LULU: He is banal. Simple minded. No education. No inkling what impression he gives. Sees nothing, neither himself nor me. Blind as a stovepipe.

SCHONING: Take him in hand.

LULU: I'm not his governess.

SCHONING: He bores you.

LULU: I'm his wife.

SCHONING: Take him in hand. That's what any wife has to do.

LULU: I didn't have to get married to be in that position.

SCHONING: You're creating illusions for yourself—about the, um, legitimate world.

LULU: I'm creating no illusions. None. —I even dream, sometimes of Dr. Goll.

SCHONING: The old magician! —He spoiled you.

LULU: He was not banal.

SCHONING: Him and his dance lessons.

LULU: Sometimes I see his fat red head above me—

SCHONING: It's his whip you want.

LULU: Every three or four nights, I dream his burial was all a misunderstanding. There he is—as if he'd never been away. Only he walks so quietly, like he had no shoes on. He's not mad at me for marrying Schwarz—only a bit sad— Otherwise he's comfortable with us—just can't get over the fact that I've thrown so much money away.

SCHONING: Desecration of corpses.

LULU: He comes of his own accord.

SCHONING: Haven't you had enough by now?

LULU: What d'you call enough...?

SCHONING: If he has no education, what about...the sacred ties of...?

LULU: He loves me.

SCHONING: A fatality.

LULU: I'm supposed to have children.

SCHONING: Love never gets beyond animalism!

LULU: I feel accused of things all the time. —He doesn't know me. Calls me a woodchuck and a gazelle and hasn't a clue who I am. He'd say the same to any girl who taught piano.

Never went after a girl in all his life. Says so himself.

SCHONING: His mouth always dropped open at the sight of an appetizing female. Ever since he was fourteen.

LULU: He still boasts of that.

SCHONING: Hm.

LULU: He's scared. At every rising of the moon, feels attacked by some secret sickness.

SCHONING: A hypochondriac.

LULU: And I'm his condom.

SCHONING: Well...

LULU: When I'm just nauseated, he thinks it's childish modesty. I see right through him at such times. And when anyone else would be shouting for joy, he's weeping bucketfuls.

SCHONING: Many an unspoiled young woman would give anything to be in your position!

LULU: He should look for one such. But he has his hands full with me. When I perfume my hair and throw on two dark pleated slips, lots of lace, bracelets round my knees...

SCHONING: I remember...

LULU: ...With just my arms uncovered...he runs wild like a Zulu, crash, bang...after which he has nothing left for me but a few snorts...

SCHONING: Unbelievable.

LULU: I dance to the tune of "ta-ra-ra-boom-de-ay" in my baby costume, and he falls asleep.

SCHONING: He's an artist all right.

LULU: Thinks he is.

SCHONING: Which is the main thing.

LULU: He also thinks he's famous.

SCHONING: I've made him so after all.

LULU: Suspicious as a thief yet lets himself be lied to and deceived. One loses all respect...On our wedding night I made him believe I was still a virgin!

SCHONING: God in heaven!

LULU: Otherwise he'd have thought me immoral.

SCHONING: You got away with that?

LULU: Hm.

SCHONING: It could be quite unpleasant...

LULU: I shouted...

SCHONING: For...

LULU: For...

SCHONING: Joy...?

LULU: He thought so.

SCHONING: So he wasn't disappointed.

LULU: He's been patting himself on the back ever since.

SCHONING: (*Getting up.*) One envies him. —I always said so.

LULU: He learned self-esteem right off, and has spoken of himself with enthusiasm ever since.

SCHONING: All of this changes nothing. (*He walks up and down.*) I still have to be on guard. Right now I cannot afford any scandal.

LULU: I'll do anything—anything to keep him happy.

SCHONING: That won't serve my purpose. I want to give my wife an immaculate home.

LULU: What are you up to with that child...?

SCHONING: It's no business of yours.

LULU: She's too young for you.

SCHONING: She's exactly three years younger than you.

LULU: She'll bore you to death. The little lady bores you when she's noisy and bores you when she's quiet.

SCHONING: She'll learn.

LULU: She'll break apart in your hands.

SCHONING: Don't stand in my way. Since you married Schwarz, I've given you no grounds to take our relationship seriously...

LULU: My God...

SCHONING: I've done everything you could ask. You have a healthy young husband. I've furthered his career. Let me

have my bit of freedom. I want to live what's left of my life.
—When you come to my place and throw your chemise in
the corner before I even know what's going on, it's hard for
me to respect the married woman in you.

LULU: You're sick of me.

SCHONING: (*Bites his lip.*)

LULU: That's all there is to it.

SCHONING: All.

LULU: (*Getting up.*) But I won't be thrown aside...

SCHONING: Here we go.

LULU: I'll hold my ground as long as there's strength in my
body...

SCHONING: Mignon...

LULU: From one day to the next, bang! it's like you'd never seen
me before.

SCHONING: It had to happen some time.

LULU: The whole world can trample me under foot, but not you.
Not you.

SCHONING: D'you want money?

LULU: I belong to you. Everything I have comes from you. Take
it back. Take me on as your maid or something.

SCHONING: I brought you up, married you off, married you off
twice. Now I want you to become a *respectable* wife.

LULU: A respectable...?

SCHONING: If you're grateful, show it.

LULU: Make of me what you wish, why else am I there? Only,
don't throw me away.

SCENE SIX. Schwarz. The foregoing.

SCHWARZ: (*Brush in hand, from the right.*) What is it, then...?

LULU: He's rejecting me! After telling me a thousand times...

SCHONING: Shut up. Shut up.

LULU:...telling me a thousand times...stammering that there was no love like mine...

SCHWARZ: (*Takes* LULU *by the arm and leads her off, right.*)

SCHONING: (*Alone.*) A bitter pill!

SCHWARZ: (*Returns, brush still in hand.*) Is that something to joke about?

SCHONING: No.

SCHWARZ: Then please explain.

SCHONING: Yes.

SCHWARZ: Yes? Yes?

SCHONING: Let's sit, I'm tired. (*He takes a chair.*)

SCHWARZ: (*Hesitating.*) What *is* this?

SCHONING: Sit down. Please.

SCHWARZ: (*Sitting.*) What *is* this? —Explain.

SCHONING: You heard.

SCHWARZ: I heard nothing.

SCHONING: You want to hear nothing.

SCHWARZ: I don't understand.

SCHONING: Be clear about what you owe her.

SCHWARZ: Oh yes, I am.

SCHONING: You married half a million Marks.

SCHWARZ: That's something she can't help.

SCHONING: You married half a million Marks.

SCHWARZ: Well, and...

SCHONING: You're wallowing in happiness.

SCHWARZ: Certainly.

SCHONING: For which you have her to thank.

SCHWARZ: Yes.

SCHONING: You were a beggar.

SCHWARZ: Yes. Yes. Has she complained about me?

SCHONING: It's not a matter of that.

SCHWARZ: She *has* complained about me!

SCHONING: Pull yourself together. We're not children.

SCHWARZ: What more does she want?

SCHONING: She wants the whip.

SCHWARZ: She has everything she wants.

SCHONING: You are...

SCHWARZ: Tell me what all this means.

SCHONING: She said it. Here. In front of your nose.

SCHWARZ: (*Turning pale.*) But she didn't want to...

SCHONING: You married half a million Marks.

SCHWARZ: Does she want to deceive me?

SCHONING: What's happened has happened, accept it.

SCHWARZ: Happened?

SCHONING: It's your fault if you were deceived.

SCHWARZ: *What* happened?

SCHONING: For six months you've lived in a seventh heaven of delight. That remains true. You have her to thank for it.

SCHWARZ: What has she done?

SCHONING: She told you.

SCHWARZ: Yes?

SCHONING: I have known her for thirteen years.

SCHWARZ: You...?

SCHONING: You've made a name for yourself. You're able to work. For which, money was required. You haven't had to deny yourself anything. You have your freedom...

SCHWARZ: You deceived me...

SCHONING: So? We should now shoot each other?

SCHWARZ: Shoot each...shoot...

SCHONING: I am taking no action.

SCHWARZ: God! God!

SCHONING: It hurts, does it?

SCHWARZ: God!

SCHONING: No one deceived you.

SCHWARZ: Then I don't understand.

SCHONING: You don't want to understand. —I came here to make an end of it.

SCHWARZ: Yes. I know.

SCHONING: I came to tell her: No further visits. —For your sake.

SCHWARZ: So then...

SCHONING: Help me appeal to her sense of duty. She doesn't know what she's doing. Doesn't know any better.

SCHWARZ: You...knew her...?

SCHONING: Yes. At seven years old, she ran from one cafe to another, barefoot, without underskirt, selling flowers.

SCHWARZ: She told me she lived with a bad tempered aunt...

SCHONING: The woman I placed her with.

SCHWARZ: Flower girl...Without underskirt...

SCHONING: *That* she didn't tell you.

SCHWARZ: No.

SCHONING: Can one blame her?

SCHWARZ: Flower girl...

SCHONING: Why do I tell you? So you won't think her depraved. All the time I've known her, she's improved, she was an excellent pupil...

SCHWARZ: How often did she...?

SCHONING: That doesn't come into it. —The house mother set her up as a model to all the other "daughters." At final exam time.

SCHWARZ: At the girls' secondary school?

SCHONING: (*Nodding.*) I have her report cards.

SCHWARZ: When I first got to know her, she told me she was still...untouched.

SCHONING: She was a widow.

SCHWARZ: She swore it...(SCHONING *gets up and walks left.*) by her mother's grave.

SCHONING: She never knew her mother, let alone her grave. Her mother has no grave.

SCHWARZ: God!

SCHONING: (*Returning.*) I didn't come here to discuss your *idées fixes.*

SCHWARZ: How long was she at that school?

SCHONING: Five years...To her schoolfellows, she was a little goddess, so enchanting, as she ran down the street with them in winter at four o'clock...The girls went home with her—to do their homework. Later, she spent six months in Lausanne...

SCHWARZ: In the boarding house?

SCHONING: Yes. In Lausanne everyone was equally taken with her. She was going to stay longer. I took her away because the headmistress fell madly in love with her.

SCHWARZ: Why didn't you tell me all this before?

SCHONING: Why, why, why didn't I tell you all this before? (*He sits opposite him.*) At the time old Goll died, the girl was closer to me than you were.

SCHWARZ: Old Goll—she says he made her dance...

SCHONING: You married half a million Marks.

SCHWARZ: Where did he get her?

SCHONING: From me.

SCHWARZ: He never even touched her...

SCHONING: He married her. How she handled it, I wouldn't know.

SCHWARZ: I saw in her...my savior!

SCHONING: And by now, surely, you know?

SCHWARZ: Know?...Yes.

SCHONING: Maybe she told him *I* never touched her.

SCHWARZ: My savior! I told myself that, that, that heaven had made her for me and me for her...

SCHONING: Dr. Goll said that too.

SCHWARZ: I was so miserable.

SCHONING: She should get the credit. —If she isn't really what you imagine, then, make her so! The error will then be all yours.

SCHWARZ: God!

SCHONING: When she married you, that also redounded to her credit.

SCHWARZ: Really?

SCHONING: You were able to make a life for yourself with her.

SCHWARZ: She'd told me she was still...

SCHONING: If you don't make a few concessions you'll get nowhere. —You *are* an oddball.

SCHWARZ:...still untouched...

SCHONING: Touched, untouched, what were *you* up to...

SCHWARZ: Without underskirt...From one cafe to another...

SCHONING:...starting something with a virgin?

SCHWARZ: She *was* one...or I won't...

SCHONING: (*Gets up and walks to the back, then returns.*) Lend me a hand—I can't see you live this way. Or her, it's not a life, it can't bear looking at. Teach her some respect. It's terrible what's happening to her. She deserves a husband *she* can respect. She deserves to be a *respectable* woman. — Afterwards you can slip behind the bed curtains with her all the more calmly...

SCHWARZ: Afterwards...

SCHONING: With ideas like yours one can't come to terms with someone of Mignon's background.

SCHWARZ: What are you getting at?

SCHONING: Her origin, her childhood...

SCHWARZ: I don't understand.

SCHONING: The *dirt* I took her from—

SCHWARZ: Took whom?

SCHONING: Your wife.

SCHWARZ: Eve...

SCHONING: I called her Mignon.

SCHWARZ: I thought—she was called—Nelly...

SCHONING: Nelly is what Dr. Goll called her...

SCHWARZ: I call her Eve...

SCHONING: What she was originally called I don't know...

SCHWARZ: Dr. Goll called her Nelly...

SCHONING: When a girl has a father like hers, it's up to you to bring a little order into her life.

SCHWARZ: Did he...

SCHONING: He is still pursuing me.

SCHWARZ: He's still alive?

SCHONING: Who...?

SCHWARZ: Her father...

SCHONING: He was here just now.

SCHWARZ: Where?

SCHONING: Here.

SCHWARZ: Here?

SCHONING: Here. In this drawing room.

SCHWARZ: Here...

SCHONING: He was just leaving when I arrived. —See those two glasses...?

SCHWARZ: She says...she says...he perished in a typhoon in the Philippines.

SCHONING: What's the matter?

SCHWARZ: (*Gripping his chest.*) A terrible pain.

SCHONING: D'you have any...Bromo Nitrate?

SCHWARZ: No.

SCHONING: Then water. Drink some water.

SCHWARZ: You have dis...dis...dishonored her—

SCHONING: How much honor was left to take away?

SCHWARZ: I'm throttled—strangled—my heart—(*Manages to get up from the chair and stagger through the room.*)—If I could only cry—oh—how I want to cry—

SCHONING: (*Holding him up.*) Be a man. You married half a million Marks. —Who does *not* prostitute himself? You have her, don't you? —the loveliest creature...

SCHWARZ: (*Straightening up.*) Let me go...

SCHONING: (*Stepping back.*) Stop. Talk talk talk won't help. Don't lose her! Take care of her! She's your life!

SCHWARZ: You're right...you're right...

SCHONING: Don't derail the train. Look. Everything depends on you. If you were happy, you lose nothing now. She's your property, let her *feel* that. What would you prefer—some irreproachable little girl without a shirt to her back? — You're a famous artist...

SCHWARZ: You...are right...(*He totters, left.*)

SCHONING: So where are you off to?

SCHWARZ: To explain to her...what her position is...(*Off, left.*)

SCENE SEVEN. Schoning. Then Lulu.

SCHONING: (*Alone.*) He must get this load off his mind before— we sing the trio. (*Pause. He looks right, then left, then right again.*) I thought he had taken her out through this door. (*Fearful groaning, left.*)

SCHONING: (*Hurries to the door and finds it locked.*) Open the door!

LULU: (*Coming in from the right.*) What is it...?

(*The groaning continues.*)

SCHONING: Open up!

LULU: (*Stepping nearer.*) That sounds so...horrifying.

SCHONING: Do you have a hatchet in the kitchen? —I don't want to kick the door in.

LULU: He'll open the door—when he's cried his heart out...

SCHONING: (*Kicking at the door.*) Open up! (*To* LULU.) Bring me a hatchet, if there is one...

LULU: Shall I send for the doctor?

SCHONING: Are you out of your mind? Heaven only knows what...

LULU: It serves you right. (*A ring from the corridor.* SCHONING *and* LULU *stare at each other.*)

SCHONING: Let me—let me take a look. (*He goes to the back but stops in the doorway.*) I can't let myself be seen...

LULU: He groans like he had a knife in him...

SCHONING: Keep calm. (*Quietly.*) Why should anyone be home?

LULU: Maybe the...art dealer...(*Another ring.*)

SCHONING: Devil take him—if we don't answer...

LULU: (*Creeping toward the door.*)

SCHONING: (*Stopping her.*) Stay where you are. —One doesn't have to rush to the door. (*He goes out, on tiptoe.*)

LULU: (*Creeps back to the locked door and listens.*)

SCENE EIGHT. Alva Schoning. The foregoing. Later Henriette.

SCHONING: (*Bringing* ALVA *in.*) Now please—be quiet...

ALVA: The—the Reichstag has been dissolved.

SCHONING: (*Softly.*) Be quiet, I said.

ALVA: (*To* LULU.) But you're pale as death.

SCHONING: (*Rattling the door handle.*) Edward! Edward! (*From inside, a hoarse death rattle.*)

LULU: God have mercy, God have...

SCHONING: (*To* LULU.) Did you bring me a hatchet?

LULU: I don't know if there is one. (*Hesitatingly, she goes off at back, left.*)

ALVA: Did he catch you *in flagrante delicto*?

SCHONING: A madman...

ALVA: A man with a soul.

SCHONING: The Reichstag has been dissolved?

ALVA: All is confusion at the newspaper office, no one knows how to handle it. (*A ring in the corridor.*)

SCHONING: (*Kicking.*) By all that's holy...(*Trying to force the latch.*) Edward...(*Both listen.*)

ALVA: Not a sound. Shall I break the door down?

SCHONING: I could do that myself. But someone might come...(*Standing up straight.*) He's not human. An oaf. An idiot.

ALVA: Hm. He's making a fool of *us*.

SCHONING: He has himself a ball—bothers himself about nothing—and lets others pay.

LULU: (*Returns with a kitchen hatchet.*) Henriette is back.

ALVA: (*Taking it over.*) Give it here. (*He sticks the hatchet between doorpost and lock.*)

LULU: (*A hand at her breast.*) We may be in for a surprise.

ALVA: (*At work.*) I'll make a tragedy out of this.

SCHONING: You've gotta get better leverage.

ALVA: Here goes. (*The lock is broken, and the door springs open.*)

ALVA: (*Both hands to his temples, staggering into the room.*) Oh, oh...!

(*Pause.*)

LULU: (*Her whole body trembling, pointing with raised hand to the door, to* SCHONING.) So that is what...

SCHONING: Keep your mouth shut. (*He wipes his brow and enters.*)

ALVA: (*In an easy chair, down right.*) Frightful, frightful, frightful!

LULU: (*Her left hand holding on to the doorpost, the right, in excitement, raised to her mouth.*) I've never seen...anything like it.

ALVA: My breakfast is turning round in my belly, I feel sick, I'll never get over it.

LULU: (*Crying out all of a sudden.*) Oh! God help me! (*Hurries to the right, grasps* ALVA *by the shoulder.*) Come. —He just bent his head back. —Oh! —Come.

ALVA: (*Struggling for control.*) Frightful. Horrible.

LULU: Come. I can't stay here. —I can't be alone.

ALVA: I can't...I'm paralyzed...

LULU: Please!...(*She takes him by the hand and leads him off on the right.*)

SCHONING: (*Coming back on the left, a bunch of keys in his hand. Blood on his sleeves. He closes the door behind him and walks shakily to the desk, sits down at it and writes two notes.*)

ALVA: (*Returning at right, sinks down in a chair.*) She's changing, she wants to change clothes.

SCHONING: (*Rings a bell, goes back left.*)

(*Henriette enters.*)

SCHONING: D'you know where Dr. Bernstein lives?

HENRIETTE: Certainly, sir. —Just round the corner.

SCHONING: Take him this note. And hurry.

HENRIETTE: And if the Herr Doktor isn't home?

SCHONING: Leave the note for him. —And this one, take it to police headquarters. Go. (*He goes to the broken door.*)

ALVA: (*Getting up.*) I must take another look at him.

SCHONING: (*Turns around in the doorway.*) Why? Follow every impulse, however impromptu? I don't like that in you.

ALVA: I'm not used to such games, I suppose I'm not case-hardened.

LULU: (*In gray dust coat and black gloves, a lacy black hat on her head, a black sunshade in her hand, from the right.*) On all sides I see—

SCHONING: Where did he keep his papers, his valuables?

LULU: I don't know...(*To* ALVA.) Come...

ALVA: You're so pretty...

SCHONING: (*Goes to the desk and opens the drawers.*)

LULU: My heart is beating like the clock in the church tower.

ALVA: I feel it in my legs. I feel quite...

LULU: Get me outta here.

SCHONING: (*At the desk.*) Damn these people.

LULU: You brought us to this pass.

SCHONING: Quiet. Or I...

LULU: You are the murderer.

SCHONING: I'm the fool...with my love for this fellow...

LULU: (*Starts to sob.*)

ALVA: (*Staring blankly before him.*) Meanwhile the poor fellow is not yet cold.

LULU: (*Weeping.*) And will never again be warm.

ALVA: So we're among ourselves. (*He sinks down in a chair.*)

SCHONING: The one concession I made in my whole life!

LULU: So?

SCHONING: This kid Schwarz has brought the house tumbling down on my head.

ALVA: How to get his story on to the stage?

LULU: (*To* SCHONING.) You can draw a veil over this matter—as over so many others.

SCHONING: How?

ALVA: Write his obit in tomorrow's paper. You knew him best. — Suppress a tear and call him another Raphael. Then no one will find you guilty of anything.

LULU: (*To* SCHONING.) Yes, write a complimentary article.

SCHONING: (*Walks up and down.*)—I see myself the subject of an editorial: DON JUAN'S VICTIM.

ALVA: (*To* LULU.) He fears for his marriage plans.

LULU: One must invent something...

SCHONING: (*To* LULU.) What are you going to tell the police?

ALVA: I'm not interested in seeing you remarry...

SCHONING: I don't care what interests you.

ALVA: Autumn sunshine. —I now face the prospect of a roomful of kids.

SCHONING: You've seen me dispose of half my fortune twice before.

ALVA: Marry your mistress.

LULU: Everything's revolving before my eyes.

ALVA: She's free again, happily—on an open sea.

SCHONING: (*Goes to the desk.*) The guy was all wrapped up in himself...

ALVA: I mean, if one *must* be married.

LULU: I see nothing but blood.

ALVA: For me, she's a firm guarantee that the family won't grow.

LULU: Who says so?

ALVA: You are a promise to that effect.

SCHONING: (*Half turning round.*) A whore.

LULU: (*Pounces on him with raised sunshade.*)

ALVA: (*Throwing himself between them.*) Calm down, both of you!

(*Leading* LULU *to the left.*) He must unburden himself somehow. —He's in love like a teenager...

SCHONING: You marry her. You'll never find anyone better. Have your plays produced with her money. Pay your girlfriends with it...

ALVA: Thank you, father dear.

SCHONING: I've had enough of her.

ALVA: I'm not under the sad compulsion to...

LULU: I don't want you. Even at death's door.

ALVA: No danger, dear lady.

SCHONING: My hair's standing on end.

ALVA: End...end...end...

SCHONING: A hangman's apprentice would fall silent at such a blow... But this dehumanized pack...

LULU: One must find one's feet somehow...

ALVA: Objectivity comes hard...for me anyway...

SCHONING: I'm not on top of this yet.

ALVA: Add that the Reichstag had been dissolved...

SCHONING: That too! —Incidental right now.

ALVA: Confusion reigns at the newspaper office. It's a tower of Babel.

SCHONING: I'm waiting for the police. —You go. I should follow in five minutes.

ALVA: I must see him once more. (*Walks to the broken-in door and opens it up.*)

LULU: (*To* SCHONING.) There's blood...

SCHONING: Where...

LULU: Wait. I'll wipe it off. (*She sprays heliotrope on a handkerchief and rubs flecks of blood off* SCHONING'*s sleeve.*)

SCHONING: It's from him.

LULU: I often saw it.

SCHONING: He bled easily?

LULU: (*Smiling.*) You can't see any now.

SCHONING: (*Through his teeth.*) What a horror!

LULU: And you'll marry *me*.

ALVA: (*In the doorway.*) Blood, blood, blood, it's ghastly.

LULU: (*Approaching the doorway.*) There was always something frightful about him.

SCHONING: (*Approaching the doorway.*) Only don't touch him, for God's sake.

LULU and ALVA: (*Together.*) God forbid.

ALVA: A crazy guy.

LULU: How can anyone do such a thing?

ALVA: With a razor.

LULU: Still in his hand.

SCHONING: That's a good thing.

ALVA: Must be a ghastly feeling...

LULU: Cutting through your throat with a razor...

ALVA: Look at the sheets—the floor—

LULU: What a mess.

ALVA: Dripping all over.

LULU: Look at his hands.

ALVA: He was always too highstrung.

SCHONING: He's showing us the way.

LULU: He had no education.

ALVA: He was behind the times.

SCHONING: He lived on credit.

SCENE NINE. Henriette. Dr. Bernstein. The foregoing.

HENRIETTE: (*Opening the door.*) Herr Doktor Bern—

DR. BERNSTEIN: (*Going to* SCHONING, *breathless.*) But how is it possible, Herr Doktor?

SCHONING: Depression...

END OF ACT TWO

LULU has married DR. SCHONING, has slept, on their wedding day, with his son ALVA, and has started an affair with the acrobat RODRIGO QUAST.

ACT THREE

Splendid room in German Renaissance style with heavy ceiling in carved oak. Dark wainscotting half way up the walls. Above this wainscotting, faded Gobelin tapestries. A gallery hung with drapes cuts off the upper half of the room toward the back of the stage. A monumental staircase comes down from this gallery to about half way from the front of the stage. Under the gallery, the entrance with a pediment supported by twisted columns. Left and right of center, downstage, heavy closed portieres made of Genoese velvet. The banister ends in a pillar in front of which stands the picture of Lulu as Pierrot. It is in an antique-style gold frame. The red beneath the gold shows through.

Downstage right, a broad ottoman. In the middle of the room, a square oak table with two highbacked upholstered chairs. —Ancient upholstered chairs, antiques, Oriental art objects, weapons, animal skins etc. A bouquet of white flowers in a porcelain vase with flamingos painted on it is on the table.

SCENE ONE. Dr. Schoning. Lulu. Countess Martha von Geschwitz. Rodrigo Quast.

GESCHWITZ is sitting on the ottoman. Her black-gloved hands are held convulsively in a muff. lulu is in the armchair to her left in a morning gown with big brightcolored flowers on it and cut very low. In her hair, tied in a simple knot, is a gold buckle. Flesh colored stockings. On her feet, white satin shoes. —schoning is standing downstage right. —RODRIGO QUAST is hidden behind the lefthand portiere.

GESCHWITZ: (*To* LULU.) How happy I am that we'll be seeing you at the Ball for Women Artists!

SCHONING: I only hope that, in her choice of costume, my wife will stay within limits?

GESCHWITZ: Rest easy. My friend's taste is much too delicate to...

SCHONING: Excuse me, Fräulein von Geschwitz, your exclusion of men from your organization prevents us journalists from finding out how far this fairy tale might go...

LULU: I'm going because I'm invited. —I'd as soon *not* go...

SCHONING: (*To* GESCHWITZ.) Is it quite impossible to smuggle us in?

GESCHWITZ: Quite impossible, Herr Doktor. The Ball for Women Artists is founded on this exclusivity. Our ladies can dance with men when they want, at this Ball they belong to us.

SCHONING: No rivalry need arise, Fräulein. I could come as a kiosk: covered with posters.

GESCHWITZ: We are inexorable.

SCHONING: Well, you've nothing to worry about from me. (*Taking out his cigarette case, to himself.*) With all due respect for my peace of mind...(*Aloud.*) Do the ladies smoke?

GESCHWITZ: (*Helping herself*). By your leave.

SCHONING: (*To* LULU.). And you, Mignon?

LULU: No thanks.

SCHONING: (*Giving* GESCHWITZ *a light.*) My wife sees smoking from an excessively aesthetic viewpoint.

LULU: But if I offer you all a liqueur?

SCHONING: No thanks.

LULU: Fräulein ?

GESCHWITZ: Oh, don't bother, just for me...

LULU: Oh, please, I have it right here. (*She goes to a small cupboard under the stairs.*)

SCHONING: (*Walking to the table.*)—Tuberoses, how magnificent! Ah! (*Smelling them.*)

LULU: Aren't they? Fräulein von Geschwitz brought them...

SCHONING: (*To* GESCHWITZ.) You'll be ruined. (*To* LULU.) It's not your birthday, however.

LULU: (*Brings forward small a Japanese table and places it in front of the sofa: the liqueurs are on it.*) My birthday? I was wondering about that.

GESCHWITZ: (*To* LULU.) Are you trying to upset me?

SCHONING: And all pure white...why is that?

LULU: (*Pouring the liqueur for* GESCHWITZ *and herself.*) I don't think I understand the language of flowers...

GESCHWITZ: My regrets, Frau Doktor, but there was nothing prettier in the store.

SCHONING: (*Walking left, to himself.*) These happened to be the prettiest...

LULU: (*Touching glasses with* GESCHWITZ.) Nothing to worry about. (*Tosses off the liqueur.*)

GESCHWITZ: (*Having taken a sip, she looks round the room:* LULU*'s picture catches her eye.*) You are charming. You are enchanting. And this is how I'd choose to see you! Is it the work of a local artist?

LULU: A certain Schwarz.

GESCHWITZ: Schwarz—I recall the name.

LULU: I hardly think you'd have known him.

GESCHWITZ: Isn't he still alive?

LULU: No.

SCHONING: He cut his throat.

LULU: *You're* in a nasty mood.

GESCHWITZ: (*To* LULU.) If he was in love with *you*—I understand.

LULU: There was something creepy about him.

GESCHWITZ: Like everyone. (*Rising.*) I must be going, Frau Doktor, we have a Life Class this evening, and I have to prepare for the Ball...

LULU: (*Accompanying her to the door.*) Thank you for coming over, dear lady.

SCHONING: (*Following them.*) Enjoy yourself—at the Ball for Women Artists.

RODRIGO: (*At left, sticks his head out of the portiere. When he catches sight of those present he bobs right back.*)

SCHONING: (*To* GESCHWITZ.) Wouldn't there be room for—couldn't you stick us in the boxes, maybe?

GESCHWITZ: (*Taking her final leave.*) Herr Dok-tor!

LULU: (*Goes out with her.*)

SCENE TWO. Schoning. Rodrigo (Behind the portiere).

SCHONING: (*Coming forward; to himself.*) My own son! (He walks to the table, takes note of the flowers, and walks right.) Soon he'll be here. (*Pulling himself together.*) I'm through, thinking it over. —In God's name, Rodrigo! (*He walks toward the left portiere and stands in front of it.*) The scandal does not scare me, it won't destroy me, people will just say I was after sensational publicity. But my house—a veritable Augean stable! —First, now, the proof. Then too, a feeling quite unfamiliar to me. I've got to fight for my life. Am I worth it? It's a matter of vital strength, how much of that do I have left? (*Noticing the table with liqueurs.*) Too bad liquor doesn't help her. She can take it in incredible quantities—

SCENE THREE. Lulu. The foregoing.

LULU: (*Returning.*) She kissed my hand...

SCHONING: Can't I see you in your costume?

LULU: No—no...

SCHONING: Yet you don't hesitate to let strangers see you...

LULU: You are no stranger.

SCHONING: I wouldn't be critical.

LULU: It isn't ready yet.

SCHONING: It's just that I'd like to see you before...

LULU: You're reproaching me!

SCHONING: You are unaccommodating.

LULU: It's Ladies Only.

SCHONING: That's what I mean.

LULU: Oh, please, please.

SCHONING: (*Walking over to the right.*) Then don't.

LULU: Where are you going?

SCHONING: They want a piece on the matinee.

LULU: You're always out.

SCHONING: Well, of course.

LULU: Why not take today off, though?

SCHONING: What his five race horses are to the Duke of Sheffield, your bare shoulders are to me. I write and write for your greater glory.

LULU: Why?

SCHONING: Because I admire *you.* —You know: one can tell the artist by what he—or she—leaves out.

LULU: Better to die than have life turn sour on you.

SCHONING: A pretty sentiment.

LULU: Dying is so easy. —At one time I was terribly afraid of it.

SCHONING: One can also live "easy."

LULU: And I want to. —Bare shoulders are the least of my worries.

SCHONING: When life ceases to be "easy"...oh, well...that's why I married you.

LULU: Because I know how to dress...?

SCHONING: Because you would make my life easier.

LULU: But you didn't marry me.

SCHONING: What did I do?

LULU: I married you.

SCHONING: (*Kissing her on the forehead.*) A rather daring enterprise.

LULU: You're leaving?

SCHONING: I have to laugh.

LULU: Then why don't you?

SCHONING: Later, later. (*Exit, right.*)

SCENE FOUR. Lulu. Rodrigo.

RODRIGO: (*On right, sticking his head out of the portiere.*) Permit me, madam...

LULU: Stay—just a moment—

RODRIGO: It's no fun. Nearly an hour by my watch. At least give me a drink.

LULU: In God's name!

RODRIGO: (*Emerges, wearing a loud, check, tightly buttoned, close fitting, sack suit, the sleeves somewhat too short, bellbottom pants, fiery, red tie, gold earrings.*)

LULU: (*Handing him a small, full glass.*) Are you worn out?

RODRIGO: I'm always worn out. —And thanks. —But if the lady has no time?

LULU: I have, I have. —Just a moment.

RODRIGO: (*Looking round.*) This place is fabulous. A period piece! Though one doesn't feel comfortable in it. —But if the lady is otherwise engaged?

LULU: If you can wait one minute...

RODRIGO: I'd like to ask for the fifty Marks.

LULU: What muscles you've got!

RODRIGO: The fifty Marks for my poor wife.

LULU: Oh, so you're married...

RODRIGO: I couldn't possibly come to her bedside with empty hands.

LULU: Wait! Please! I must just...

RODRIGO: The lady is not well?

LULU: Quite well. Fresh as a daisy. It's just, I have to think of many...

RODRIGO: (*Shyly taking her by the waist.*) Think of my poor wife!

LULU: (*Pushing him back.*) One minute. Please!

RODRIGO: Hm. If you say so. —Give me another drink.

LULU: (*Pouring him one.*) He may come back. What a disaster after we'd waited so long!

RODRIGO: Might I suggest meeting in future at the Lorelei Tavern? Where this On-the-Qui-Vive business won't apply? It's all very luxurious here, and the drinks sure leave nothing to be desired, but, for a successful affair, madam, a high degree of security is required.

LULU: One is so *in*secure.

RODRIGO: Give me the fifty Marks. And write to me.

LULU: One second. It's nicer here. Nice and cool.

RODRIGO: Give me another drink.

LULU: (*Recoiling.*) God help me!

RODRIGO: And God punish *me*. There's some *other* fellow?

LULU: (*Pushing him, left.*) Behind the drape! —I saw this coming.

RODRIGO: Give me the fifty Marks and let me out!

LULU: (*Opening the portiere.*) Come.

RODRIGO: Awright, make it twenty.

LULU: Come on! In God's name!

RODRIGO: Get me out of here!

LULU: D'you want him to shoot you down?

RODRIGO: (*Disappears behind the portiere.*)

LULU: (*Closing the curtain.*) You're out of your mind.

SCENE FIVE. Schoning. The foregoing.

SCHONING: (*From the right, markedly pale.*) I forgot—

LULU: (*Motionless, behind the table.*) Your opera glasses?

SCHONING: (*Goes back, left, talking to himself with a glance at* LULU.) He's here already. (*Opens an incrusted casket, takes out two small envelopes, places one in his breast pocket, and comes forward with the smaller one.*)—What did the Countess want, actually?

LULU: Don't know. —She wants to paint me.

SCHONING: (*To himself.*) I'm trembling like an aspen leaf.

LULU: She gives me the creeps.

SCHONING: (*Down left, has opened the smaller envelope and, turning away, has given himself an injection under his left cuff.*) Me too. She gives *me* the creeps.

LULU: You shouldn't be doing that.

SCHONING: She's misery personified—misery lying in wait for someone.

LULU: You'd promised me not to, ever.

SCHONING: That's why I locked it up.

LULU: You are nothing to me now.

SCHONING: I did try.

LULU: It will kill you.

SCHONING: (*To himself.*) Thanks to you.

LULU: Then drink—

SCHONING: (*Closing the envelope and fastening his cuff, with a sigh.*) I guess I'll dine at Peter's Place. (*He puts his hat on.*)

LULU: (*Falls on his neck, and kisses him.*)

SCHONING: (*Gently pulling free.*) No, no, you're a well-bred girl, we all know that. (*Pressing her hand.*) Till this evening.

LULU: (*Goes with him to the doorway, listens.*)

RODRIGO: (*Sticks his head out of the portiere.*)

LULU: (*Signals to him to get back.*)

SCENE SIX. Alva. Lulu. Rodrigo Quast. Later Schoning, Ferdinand, Schigolch.

ALVA: (*In a dazzling smart get-up, opera hat in hand, walks to the doorway and folds* LULU *in his arms.*) At last, at last!

RODRIGO: (*Withdraws behind the portiere.*)

LULU: (*Her whole body trembling.*) God in Heaven!

ALVA: (*Bringing her forward.*) I was hiding outside the door.

LULU: I wish I were a hundred miles away.

ALVA: With me here?

LULU: Oh, if you only knew—*I* hardly know, myself—I'm so unspeakably miserable—if you only knew...

ALVA: But you begged me to come. You promised me everything.

You set me on fire, you fired my innermost being!

LULU: For Heaven' s sake, stay. You're the only one I can talk to. You're so dear to me—*He* ground his teeth as he left like there was a pebble in his mouth.

ALVA: Hemorrhoids, hemorrhoids! Don't tell me about it. His self-conceit borders on the monstrous, but I can't be jealous: what is he to me? So much wind. —I know who you belong to. I can *feel* you—on horseback, sitting in the Eden Cafe, lying on the sofa, I feel YOU there. You. Your body.

LULU: It's yours. It's going to be yours. But tranquilize me, narcotize me, or I'll never make it. (*Looking left.*) You hear nothing?

ALVA: Deathly quiet.

LULU: But I feel someone is listening.

ALVA: You're not well?

LULU: I'm fresh as a daisy. For fourteen days now I've been...chaste. I don't know that it is...

ALVA: Why did you invite me over? You said we'd have a Bacchanalian Revel, and I got into this class outfit.

LULU: (*Sinking into his gaze.*) You are so handsome.

ALVA: Full evening dress.

LULU: To love you like this, and then to die!

ALVA: (*Receiving this in the stomach.*) Oh!

LULU: I've set it all up, a small supper. If only there weren't all this excitement.

ALVA: Stop, or I'll explode. You don't seem to notice *I'm* here! The state I'm in: what with the rough cab ride coming over, I got here panting with my tongue hanging out. You offered me a Mini-Orgy, remember? "A Mini-Orgy Awaits You!" In bed, for these last nights, it's been like you were right there at my side and now: here I am! Here you are! I see every movement of your body. I see your glowing eyes. Under that floral design, I can make out your knees. So, unless you intend to make a sex murderer of me, I must give immediate expression to the ecstasy I feel!

LULU: Rather important right now—

ALVA: What could be important NOW? I'm dying of starvation and you're enjoying my final convulsions!

LULU: I love hearing you talk like this.

ALVA: What do I get in return? (*Taking her to the ottoman.*) Am I too plainspoken? I came here by cab...

LULU: To fall into the hands of a sex murderer could be interesting.

ALVA: What was it you wanted to chat about?

LULU: The Women Artists' Ball. If only they really were artists. They invited me three times over. Geschwitz just left. She wants to paint me. After all, I told myself—you're not listening! —the best idea is to dress as simply as possible... (SCHONING *appears in the gallery between the pillars on the right above the stairs. He pushes the curtains aside somewhat.*)

ALVA: As simply as possible...

LULU: This morning, coming from my bath, I rehearsed—my hair in a plain knot with a clasp—

ALVA: Like now?

LULU: Exactly.

ALVA: Charming!

LULU: I left it that way. It made me feel like slipping between my own legs, oh yes, as I looked in the mirror I understood Geschwitz! I wish I'd been a man at some point—a man focussed on me: think of having ME between the pillows!

ALVA: (*Viscerally.*) Oh!

LULU: Otherwise I'm glad I'm NOT a man. Better, this way, and kissable all over!

ALVA: (*Burying his head in her bosom.*) Your fantasies send the blood running from my eyes. —Katya! —Warm flexible flesh under delicate silk! —Can't feel any chemise or stiff underclothing: wherever, whatever one feels is you, just you: always slender but now the perfection of womanhood with, still, the small breasts of a girl. —So appetizing: the way you got yourself up for me, Katya, I need that kind of thing. Flowing silk on every slope, round every curve—!

LULU: (*Burying her fingers in his hair.*) This is only my morning gown...

ALVA: A man could creep inside it and make love to you, the silk in his fingers—

LULU: It's for my Lord and Husband...

ALVA: That scoundrel...

LULU: That's why it's cut so broad...

ALVA: Not TOO broad to...

LULU: Men like to see a little bit of heaven...

ALVA: Not TOO broad, Katya...

LULU: Men are astronomers.

ALVA: It's not too broad, not at all...(*He starts to unbutton from the top.*)

LULU: (*Throws her arms back and smiles away to herself.*)

ALVA: (*Uncovering an elf costume under the morning gown.*) What?! I'm going mad! —What?! —I'm hallucinating.

LULU: (*Quickly stands up. now the gown lies on the divan.*) This is for you! (*She is now in bright silk tights and a sleeveless, pale red, silk blouse divided down to the waist back and front, tightly belted, cut off high over the hips on both sides, narrowing down back and front, and closed between the legs. White satin shoes. Dark roses at her bosom.*)
(SCHONING *in the gallery lets down the curtain and disappears.* ALVA *has slid to the floor and is pressing* LULU's *feet to his lips.*)

ALVA: It'll all dissolve before my eyes. That's what I fear: I daren't look up, it'll disappear at the first touch. I can't bear it: you grab me in the gut, Katya, in the spine. I'm gonna have an apoplectic fit. Oh, Katya, Katya...

LULU: (*Trying to pull free.*) Ow! Ow! You're biting me.

ALVA: I won't let go of these feet—these tiny bones—this gentle swelling—Every inch a...a...what a knee, Merciful God! This proudly girlish *Capriccio*—between the *Andante* of Desire and the unspeakably tender *Cantabile* of these calves! What calves! Voices of children in my ears! Embracing you, every finger tip pulsates with—I don't think I can stand up.

LULU: (*Touching his shoulders.*) You won't have to. (*She walks to the back and rings the bell.*) Come.

ALVA: (*Dragging himself to the table with difficulty.*) My head's so empty you'd think I'd just killed sixteen bottles of champagne.

LULU: (*Sitting opposite.*) You're my good angel come to light up my soul.

(ALVA *at left of table,* LULU *at right.* RODRIGO, *behind* ALVA, *sticks his head out of the portiere.* LULU *gives him a furious glance.* RODRIGO *goes back.* FERDINAND *enters with a tray, sets the table for two, serving cold partridge pie with a bottle of Pommery on ice.*)

LULU: (*Rubbing her hands.*) I've arranged things the way you wanted.

ALVA: (*Taking charge of the bottle.*) I don't know if I can summon the necessary appetite. (FERDINAND *places the napkin on his arm, glances at the table, and withdraws through the middle door.*)

ALVA: But I *am* thirsty.

LULU: (*Referring to* FERDINAND.) He is discreet.

ALVA: (*Filling the glasses.*) I'm a soul in heaven, rubbing the sleep from his eyes.

LULU: (*Hands between knees.*) I'm a butterfly slipping out of its skin.

ALVA: (*Moving in close.*) Your eyes shimmer like the water in a deep well when a stone falls into it.

LULU: (*Her glass to her lips.*) You've been turning up the ends of your moustache?

LULU: (*Passing a truffle from her plate to* ALVA*'s.*) I couldn't make love to a man who didn't dress right—in every detail.

ALVA: If, for example, he wore a Jaeger shirt...

LULU: Such a man had better strangle me, not make love to me.

ALVA: Embroidered swallow-tail coat. The Order of Saint Michael. A fancy sword. And when he wants to look human, a woolen Jaeger shirt.

LULU: With rubber ruffles. Looking like a Ceylonese.

ALVA: He doesn't wear them now?

LULU: Rubber ruffles?

ALVA: Jaeger shirts.

LULU: How can you ask?

ALVA: You should know, my charming little whore.

LULU: You are all my happiness.

ALVA: (*Again, from the gut.*) Oh, Katya! (*He rings. Pause.* FERDINAND *comes in with a plate of asparagus and changes plates.*)

ALVA: You're sweating

FERDINAND: No, no, sir.

LULU: Leave him—

FERDINAND: One is only human.

ALVA: Bring us another bottle.

FERDINAND: (*Taking away the partridge pie.*) Very well, sir. (SCHONING *appears in the gallery between the two middle pillars, cautiously opening the curtains. He takes up a position behind the balustrade and cleans his opera glasses.*)

ALVA: I'm gradually waking up. —Your plate...?

LULU: (*Passes her plate and fills the glasses.*)

ALVA: (*Serving her.*) You overwhelm me.

LULU: You say so.

ALVA: If you'd only let me get a word in.

LULU: I do, I do.

ALVA: I'll deliver a real eulogy.

LULU: I'll listen with trembling lips.

ALVA: You'd grab me by the hair.

LULU: (*Laughs.*)

ALVA: Now I can see you in detail. Your little hands fingering the asparagus. I never saw such thick asparagus, by the way.

LULU: I was almost afraid to pick it up.

ALVA: Between your bare shoulders, the head of the god Eros!

LULU: This is how I always want to be. So free in the legs, so cool in the head.

ALVA: Your very tongue revels in all this.

LULU: (*Taking the piece of asparagus from her mouth.*) See it rear up?

ALVA: (*Sinking down.*) You're driving me crazy.

LULU: Eat. Please.

ALVA: (*Rising.*) One kiss.

LULU: (*Pushing him back.*) Shame, shame!

ALVA: One kiss. A kiss!

LULU: Supper with a lady has its protocol.

ALVA: Supper with a lady? It's the LAST supper before a walk to the gallows!

LULU: (*Giving him her hand across the table.*) You're gonna have to grow up, little man.

ALVA: (*Showers kisses on her hands. Separating the middle from the ring finger, he kisses the interstice.*)

LULU: There's butter on my fingers.

ALVA: (*Sinks to his knees, lifts her bare arm above his head and kisses her armpit.*)

LULU: Now you're getting me excited—

ALVA: Caviar, caviar!

LULU: (*Pushing him back to his place.*) So be reasonable. (*She gives him her full glass.*) Knock it down. (*She wipes her fingers on the napkin.*) There's something else to come. (*She rings.*)

ALVA: What are three dozen oysters in the balance? (FERDINAND *enters, changes plates, serves roast quail with mushrooms and salad, brings two bottles of Pommery and uncorks one.*)

LULU: Make the coffee good and hot.

FERDINAND: You can count on me, madam, I hope you know that.

LULU: (*To* ALVA.) Shall we drink this in the winter garden?

ALVA: No.

LULU: (*To* FERDINAND.) In the bedroom.

FERDINAND: With rum, arrac, whisky, curaçao?

LULU: (*To* ALVA.) Rum or whisky?

ALVA: Both, please.

FERDINAND: You sure can rely on me, madam.

ALVA: (*To* FERDINAND.) You are trembling?

LULU: Let him be.

FERDINAND: I still haven't got used to this line of work.

ALVA: The things one finds out about in this world!

LULU: Leave him alone.

FERDINAND: I usually serve as coachman. (*Leaves with the asparagus.*)

SCHONING: (*In the gallery but speaking out front.*) Him too!

ALVA: (*Dismembering a quail.*) And with such delicacies you hold my lust in check! —The aroma is so suggestive—I see myself marching at the head of a column of workers! This meat is byzantine, preternatural—But your—

LULU: Flesh? (RODRIGO *sticks his head out of the portiere. When he sees* SCHONING *sitting in the gallery he is horrified and bounces back.*)

SCHONING: (*As above.*) And there's another!

LULU: (*Giving* ALVA *some salad.*) If you could only come with me to the ball. The women are all after me like hunting dogs.

ALVA: (*Pointing.*) What's this—not celery?

LULU: No?

ALVA: (*Falling apart, his strength collapsing.*) Don't you have a soul? A single spark? You are drawing the bowstring so tight it'll break. —God have mercy on my poor body, I'm shattered for life. (*He slips off his chair and embraces her knees.*) Come, death, come, death! —I'm through with staring into those two scary eyes! —I'm hardly human any more—I warn you, Katya, I warn you—

LULU: (*Letting his head slip between her knees.*) Your temples are on fire.

ALVA: (*Murmuring.*) My strength's giving out. But I've drunk suffering to the dregs. Rescue me before it's too late! Your body's so chaste, so...all lust dissolves at your touch I'm shaken to my foundations—you're not a woman—you're all warm silken loops.

LULU: Stand up.

ALVA: I can't.

LULU: Let's finish eating.

ALVA: I can't eat.

LULU: Come on over—

ALVA: (*Suddenly letting loose.*) Shut your trap!

LULU: (*Continuing.*)—Into my room.

ALVA: You nutmeg grater, you open sewer, you cloaca, you spittoon, you snot-covered hanky, cesspool, screwing machine, shitcart, craphole...

LULU: (*Steps back trembling, sees* SCHONING *sitting in the gallery.*) His father. He'll box his ears.

SCHONING: (*Has suddenly got up and closed the curtains.*)

ALVA: (*Lies motionless with his hands folded on his head.*)

LULU: (*Takes one of the roses from her breast and sticks it in her hair. She goes to the stairs and, half way up, leans against the balustrade, one foot on top of the other, her bare arms spread along the velvet-upholstered banister.*) This is the high point of my life.

SCHONING: (*Revolver in hand, entering at center, sees* ALVA *lying on the carpet and kicks his behind.*) Out!

ALVA: You?!

SCHONING: Out!

ALVA: This is something!

SCHONING: Wanna get shot?

ALVA: (*Grinning at him.*) Idealists! Moralists! Knights of the Holy Order of Impotence

SCHONING: I can shoot you down, you know.

LULU: (*Out front.*) But he won't!

ALVA: (*Who has got up.*) That'd be one way to get revenge.

SCHONING: Out!

ALVA: Congratulations!

SCHONING: Am I complaining?

ALVA: Your books may be less boring in future. You can now try writing something with blood in its veins.*

SCHONING: I shall now throw you out.

ALVA: (*Retreating.*) You and your Teutonic Tragedies!

SCHONING: You and your cheap imitations thereof! (*Grabbing him by the collar.*) This is the real thing. (*He drags him out. The door closes behind them.*)

RODRIGO: (*Rushes out of the portiere, hurries diagonally across the room, stumbles on the stairway.*)

LULU: (*Blocking his path.*) Where are you going?

RODRIGO: Out.

LULU: Where to?

RODRIGO: Let me out.

LULU: You can't leave me alone.

RODRIGO: I'll throw you over the balustrade.

LULU: You'll be running straight into his arms.

RODRIGO: (*Dropping to his knees.*) Dear lady, please, PLEASE, get me outta here! You invite me over for a bottle of champagne and then stick me behind your drapes while this lunatic fools with a pistol and you two fill your bellies with partridges. I can't even see what he's shooting at! So let me outta here or—

LULU: He's coming...

RODRIGO: (*Falling back into the room.*) Holy assholes! (*Looks around.*) How do I get out of this hell hole? He'll blow my brains out. What have I done to deserve this? (SCHONING *can now be heard approaching.*).

LULU: He shoots to kill. (RODRIGO *vanishes under the table—with the cloth, plates, et cetera on it.* SCHONING *returns, goes with*

* In the German original, Alva here calls his father "Heyse" and "Scheffel", authors he regards as stuffy and old hat.

raised pistol to the portiere, tears it open.)

SCHONING: (*To* LULU, *still on the stairs.*) Where's he gone?

LULU: Out.

SCHONING: Out where?

LULU: Out the window.

SCHONING: Over the balcony?

LULU: He's an acrobat.

SCHONING: I didn't know that. (*He goes back and locks the door.*)

RODRIGO: (*Snatching the plate of quail from the table, he disappears under the table cloth.*)

SCHONING: Let me look at you.

LULU: (*Coming down the stairs and pointing to the table set, as it is, with a cloth etc.*) This was not for you.

SCHONING: I value my luck all the more.

LULU: (*Brushing her hair back from her brow.*) You find it daring?

SCHONING: You have charm.

LULU: You notice.

SCHONING: You've come to us from the far side of the sunset.

LULU: Alone I did it!

SCHONING: On a flying trapeze.

LULU: An *elf* was more what I had in mind.

SCHONING: Were it not for your big, round, little-girl eyes, the way you move your hips would create a major scandal.

LULU: Is it better to conceal one's hips with fancy French hose? One may prefer to show them off: It's nobler.

SCHONING: Beauty conquers shamelessness. Your very flesh signifies *self*-conquest.

LULU: My very flesh IS Lulu.

SCHONING: Though maybe a corset helps.

LULU: I don't wear stays of any kind.

SCHONING: I apologize.

LULU: I feel I'm just right.

SCHONING: You don't have butterfly wings.

LULU: Butterfly wings would be overdoing it.

SCHONING: One doesn't miss them: You have such a fine swing to your legs.

LULU: And how'd you like my coiffure?

SCHONING: You plan to wear it that way at the Women Artists' Ball?

LULU: Don't you like it?

SCHONING: You'll wear it that way at the Ball?

LULU: I'll wear it this way at the Ball.

SCHONING: Aren't you ashamed?

LULU: They'll tear me to pieces.

SCHONING: So aren't you ashamed?

LULU: No.

SCHONING: I'm an old fool.

LULU: You're a...(*As she takes him to the ottoman.*) What do you want?

SCHONING: (*Sitting.*) I want you to cheer me up.

LULU: So put the gun away.

SCHONING: It's not in the way.

LULU: (*On his knee.*) Give it to me.

SCHONING: That's why I brought it. (*He gives her the gun.*)

LULU: (*Stretches out her arm and fires a shot into the ceiling.*)

SCHONING: Don't be silly.

LULU: What a noise it makes!

SCHONING: It's fully loaded.

LULU: (*Looking at it.*) It's cute.

SCHONING: It can never be cute enough for such an enchanting Devil as yourself.

LULU: And what should I be doing with it?

SCHONING: Shooting yourself. Dead.

LULU: (*Stands up and adjusts her blouse.*) If you'd also brought your riding whip...

SCHONING: No children's games, please

LULU: It would have led you to different conclusions.

SCHONING: (*Taking hold of her by the waist.*) Give me one more kiss.

LULU: (*On his knee, she flings his arms about her neck and kisses him.*) Then leave the gun out of it.

SCHONING: These lips, these lips.

LULU: (*Kisses him.*)

SCHONING: They get ever more voluptuous.

LULU: (*Kisses him.*) No gun.

SCHONING: But you need it.

LULU: (*Kisses him.*) Please.

(*Pause.*)

SCHONING: This is how it's been since we met.

LULU: Then why didn't *you* do it?

SCHONING: Because I'd've landed in jail.

LULU: You love me too much to do it.

SCHONING: For you it will be easier.

LULU: Please! Don't look at me like that.

SCHONING: Quiet, dear heart.

LULU: Everything's going black before my eyes.

SCHONING: (*Stroking her.*) Be good.

LULU: (*Yawns.*)

SCHONING: Press it against your breast.

LULU: It's still warm.

SCHONING: Now: fire!

LULU: (*Tries to, several times.*)

SCHONING: With the index finger. (*He tries to guide her hand.*)
    (LULU *lets the weapon drop with a gasp.*)

SCHONING: I've messed up again.

LULU: (*Lays her head back and rubs her knees together.*)

SCHONING: It 'd all be over by now, goose.

LULU: (*With a sigh of relief.*) And I'd be lying in the tomato sauce.

SCHONING: (*Who, unnoticed, has taken back the gun.*) Your legs, your legs...

LULU: They've gone to sleep on me.

SCHONING: Those sweet rivals.

LULU: Everyone calls them that!

SCHONING: They snuggle up to each other, each quite certain that the other is more beautiful.

LULU: (*Stretching her feet out.*) Tie them together.

SCHONING: For as soon as the She Devil is aroused—

LULU: They come apart.

SCHONING: Jealous cavaliers.

LULU: Something else. Tie me up! Whip me! —

SCHONING: Nothing doing.

LULU: Till you draw blood. I won't scream. I'll bite on a handkerchief.

SCHONING: Too late. Too late.

LULU: (*Letting her hand glide over his gray hair.*). So why don't you just forgive me?

SCHONING: I forgave you long ago, I was a father to you, always. Now more than ever.

LULU: I'm going to get dressed and have the horses harnessed. Then: together to the opera!

SCHONING: It's *Pagliacci* tonight.* (*Pause.*)—You're racking your brains to find a way out.

LULU: (*Pressing against his chest.*) Let me go, let me go.

SCHONING: If you're stronger—

LULU: Let me go, I have to go to the bathroom.

SCHONING: Is it worth the effort?

LULU: (*Stares at the floor.*)

SCHONING: You know where you have to go.

LULU: I can't...even consider it.

SCHONING: Imagine you're in the arms of...(*He kisses her passionately.*).

LULU: Not yet, not yet, I'm too young.

SCHONING: Give me your hand.

---

* The Jack the Ripper murders, invoked in Act V, took place four years before the world premiere of Pagliacci (1892), but what did Wedekind care? The reference is highly ironic here because in Pagliacci a jealous husband kills both wife and lover.

LULU: This breaks my heart.

SCHONING: Oh, come on, it won't hurt.

LULU: (*Taking the gun.*). It'll kill me.

SCHONING: Take it easy.

LULU: Animals are allowed to—After this, I'm nothing.

SCHONING: It's getting you drunk...

LULU: (*In a burst of sobs.*) Why leave the world so soon? I'm so happy—so happy—why must I—I've lived—why must I—animals are allowed to live—animals—allowed—I did what others did—I'm a woman—I'm *woman*—I'm twenty years old—

SCHONING: Bosh.

LULU: (*Positioning the gun at her breast.*) God have mercy on me.

SCHONING: (*Propelling her upwards with his knees.*) You are boring.

LULU: Everything's going black before my eyes.

SCHONING: (*Directing her hand under the left breast.*) Why spend so much time thinking it over?

LULU: (*Her eyes gaping wide.*) I'm ready now.

SCHONING: I've never seen you this way before.

LULU: Ready.

SCHONING: Now.

LULU: After which I'll be a corpse.

SCHONING: Damn you. (*He tears her away from his knees and throws her against the ottoman. Walks left excitedly.*) Damn it all.

LULU: (*Lying in front of the ottoman, pressing the gun against her breast, screaming, sobbing.*) I can't. I still can't. Oh, my life.

SCHONING: (*Returns.*)

LULU: (*Partly raising herself up, her face contorted, still with the gun at her breast.*) Be patient with me. Please. One moment of patience. I'll get to it. (*She slides against his knees.*) Please!

SCHONING: (*Nervously stamping his foot.*) Now!

LULU: (*Banging her forehead on the floor.*) I can't, I can't, I can't?

(*Doubled up.*) Can't even consider—Night, night, night, God. (*Still banging.*) Oh, oh, oh...

SCHONING: (*Uncertain, suddenly pale.*) You aren't able...?

LULU: Dark night. —When the moment comes, I'll shoot myself through the heart.

SCHONING: (*Left, at the proscenium arch, stammering.*) Must I...?

LULU: No, no, no...

SCHONING: (*Opening an envelope, he gives himself a morphine injection.*)

LULU: I'm *going* to...now! (*She raises her head.*)

SCHONING: Going to...?

ALVA: (*Emerges in silence from the curtain on the gallery stairs, wringing his hands.*)

RODRIGO: (*Comes out from under the table cloth and seizes* SCHONING's *arm.*) Look out! (*Two shots are heard.*)

SCHONING: (*Falling forward.*) I—

RODRIGO: (*Catching him.*) I was just telling you—

SCHONING: (*Spitting blood.*) I sure got mine.

LULU: (*Having jumped up, hurries up the stairs, clinging to* ALVA.)

RODRIGO: (*Carrying* SCHONING *to the ottoman.*) What a miscalculation, how could you? (*Showing his right hand which is streaming with blood.*) I got my share. (*Lays* SCHONING *down on the ottoman.*) Wait. I'll get the doctor.

SCHONING: (*His mouth open.*) No. Stay here.

(*Pause.*)

LULU: (*Approaching on tiptoe.*) Have I hurt you?

SCHONING: (*Glancing at* LULU.) I'm on fire. Get to safety. Safety. Keys. Take my keys. From the pocket.

LULU: You feel nothing.

SCHONING: Money drawer. 16,000. Lose no time. Water! Give me water. Glass of...Please.

LULU: I can't leave you like this.

SCHONING: Elf. My elf.

RODRIGO: Drink some champagne, dear sir.

SCHONING: If there is...

RODRIGO: (*Has filled a goblet from the open bottle of champagne and brought it over.*)

SCHONING: Thirsty. Thirsty.

LULU: (*Taking the glass from* RODRIGO.) Let me. (*She kneels and puts the glass to* SCHONING*'s lips.*)

SCHONING: My little elf. (*Drinking.*) Still here. Now—

LULU: It'll get you drunk.

SCHONING: (*After drinking it all.*) Oh, oh. The burning. I'm dried up. My tongue, tongue—

RODRIGO: (*Uncorking the still unopened bottle.*) Drink. That was just your first glass, now drink all you can...

(ALVA *is approaching the ottoman.*)

SCHONING: "You too, my son."

ALVA: Julius Caesar.

SCHONING: I see it now—intrigue—nearest and dearest, you—

RODRIGO: (*Filling the glass and giving it to* SCHONING.) Let's go, let's go, a good swig!

SCHONING: There's blood in it.

RODRIGO: My blood.

SCHONING: I'm dreaming.

RODRIGO: It's not poison. (*To* LULU.) Would the lady be so kind?

LULU: (*To* RODRIGO, *taking bottle and glass from him.*) I swear to God I didn't see you.

RODRIGO: (*Bandaging his hand with a handkerchief.*) It's nothing.

SCHONING: You're an...acrobat—

RODRIGO: Horizontal bar and rings, mainly. (*To* LULU.) Keep filling up.

LULU: (*Doing so.*) You can't blame it on me.

SCHONING: My elf. My murderess.

RODRIGO: (*To himself.*) It just grazed the hand.

LULU: I almost managed...to kill myself.

SCHONING: Better. It's getting better.

ALVA: Shall I send for the doctor?

SCHONING: Take—keys—my pocket—I can't move—don't touch me you know the...papers—my mother...she didn't know...merciful—one summer...month—summ—oh...

LULU: (*Kissing him.*) Look at us, look at us, you don't see us.

SCHONING: Still afraid?...Heartburn. Morphine, morphine, morph—

RODRIGO: Give him more champagne.

LULU: (*Does so.*) I almost shot myself...

SCHONING: Get to safety, all of you, you're done for...Doctor. No doctor. —I'll provide...money, money for you all—bridge—to build a bridge over the...the...isthmus...one is... (*Groaning.*) Oh...

LULU: It goes right through you.

SCHONING: Yes, yes. Kiss me just once more.

LULU: (*With her right hand on his heart, bends over and kisses him.*)

RODRIGO: (*To* ALVA.) The color of his face. All bleached out. I hope I never get to look like that, for God's sake. But what a reward: those kisses, something to take with him into the next world. Kisses on his last voyage! I'll be lucky if someone sticks a cigar in my mouth, how about you?

ALVA: Where did you come from?

RODRIGO: The café.

(*Pause.*)

LULU: (*Raising her head.*) He is dead.

ALVA: My father.

RODRIGO: (*To everyone.*) With your permission I'll excuse myself. Otherwise I'm all too likely to be the suspect.

ALVA: Place the gun in his hand while there's time.

RODRIGO: That won't help very much, sir. I don't know your line of work but he can't very well have shot himself in the back.

LULU: I'm leaving for Paris. (*To* ALVA.) Get the keys, fast.

ALVA: (*Emptying* SCHONING*'s pockets.*) What will you do in Paris?

SCHONING: (*Tonelessly.*) A bridge—

ALVA: (*Retreating.*) How ghastly.

LULU: Quiet.

RODRIGO: He's far away now. In intensive care, huh? Sounds that way.

ALVA: (*Keys in hand.*) You've gotta take me with you...

LULU: I've gotta change my clothes.

ALVA: Otherwise you won't get a penny.

LULU: I can't stop you going to Paris.

ALVA: You wouldn't want to leave me here in misery?

LULU: Give me that gown.

ALVA: You are my fate.

LULU: Give me that gown.

ALVA: All right.

LULU: He's lying on it.

ALVA: It's covered with blood (*Pulling the morning gown from under* SCHONING *and throwing it to* LULU.) I can't figure a life without you.

RODRIGO: Madam is getting blood on her tights.

LULU: No matter, I'm taking them off.

ALVA: I'm emptying the safe. Then we lock up.

LULU: (*In the doorway at right.*) The train leaves at eight.

ALVA: For Paris.

RODRIGO: I hear something.

SCHIGOLCH: (*Enters in the middle of the gallery, parting the curtains.*) It smells of human blood.

ALVA: (*His knees buckling.*) Who is this?

LULU: My father.

END OF ACT THREE

Paris, 1885. LULU has married ALVA SCHONING, and has had an affair with the MARQUIS CASTI-PIANI, white-slave trafficker.

ACT FOUR

Paris, roomy salon in white stucco. In the back wall, a broad double door. Beside this, on both sides, large mirrors. Two doors on each of the two side walls. Between these doors, on the right a rococo console with white marble top and over it a large mirror; on the left a white marble fireplace with LULU*'s picture as Pierrot above it in a narrow gold frame let into the wall. In the middle of the salon a slender, brightly upholstered Louis XV sofa. Broad, brightly upholstered armchairs with thin legs and slender arm rests. Downstage left, a small table.*

SCENE ONE.

The center door is open, revealing a broad baccarat table surrounded by upholstered Turkish chairs. ALVA SCHONING, RODRIGO QUAST, THE MARQUIS *Casti Piani, the banker* PUNTSCHUH, *the journalist* HEILMANN, LULU, COUNTESS GESCHWITZ, MADELAINE DE MARELLE. KADÉGA DI SANTA CROCE. BIANETTA GAZIL, LUDMILLA STEINHERZ *are engaged in lively conversation in the Salon. The gentlemen are in formal attire.* LULU *wears a white Directoire gown with wide puffed sleeves and white lace falling freely from the seam of a high waist. Arms in white kid gloves. Hair up. With a small plume of white feathers.* GESCHWITZ *in a pale blue hussar's jacket, edged with fur and with facings of silver braid. White bow tie, tight stand-up collar and stiff cuffs with huge ivory cuff links.* MADELAINE DE MARELLE *in an iridescent chatoyant dress of shot silk with very broad sleeves, long tight bodice and three flounces made up, spirally, of intertwined pinks, ribbons, and bunches of violets. Her hair is parted in the middle, falls low over her temples and is curled at the sides. On her brow, a pearl ornament, held in place by a small chain that passes under her hair.* KADÉGA DI SANTA CROCE, *her twelve-year-old daughter, in light green satin booties over which her white silk socks peep out. Her upper body in white lace. Pale green, close fitting sleeves; pearl-gray kid gloves. Black hair loose under a big pale-green lace hat with white feathers. BIANETTA GAZIL in dark green velvet, a collar bedecked with pearls, blouse sleeve, full skirt without waist, the hem bedecked with imitation topazes set in silver. LUDMILLA STEINHERZ in a garish blue and red striped seaside outfit. ARMANDE and BOB are serving champagne, ARMANDE in a close fitting black dress of right-angle cut with a white fichu Marie Antoinette. BOB, fourteen years old, in short red coat, taut leather pants and gleaming top boots.*

MADELAINE*: Mais c'est impossible, je ne peux pas le croire, it's crazy: life was all waltzing, gaming, horseback riding, wild, wild carrying on. And now it's over?

BIANETTA: I was only there once—with the old Duc de Brétigny, my lover at the time—

RODRIGO: (*A full glass in his hand.*) Mesdames et Messieurs, excuse the interruption, Mesdames et Messieurs, but it is the birthday of our beloved hostess Madame la Comtesse who has brought us together this evening. To the health of Countess Adelaide d'Oubra! Drink to the health of...(*They all surround* LULU *and drink to*: Madame la Comtesse!)

RODRIGO: I live again!

ALVA: (*Pressing his hand.*) Congratulations.

RODRIGO: I know I am not French like you all...

BIANETTA: Where DO you come from, by the way?

RODRIGO: I am...Austrian.

BIANETTA: And you lift weights, Monsieur Quast?

RODRIGO: Exactly, Madame de Marelle.

MADELAINE: I don't care for athletes. I prefer marksmen. There was a marksman at the Casino, and every time he went

---

* In Wedekind's original, the French characters speak in French. But one cannot ask a British or American audience to accept this, and little of the French has been held over in this adaptation.

BOOM I...(*She quivers from head to foot.*)

BIANETTA: But look, ma chère, he doesn't have the hands of a weight lifter. See (*And she places her hand in* RODRIGO*'s.*)! My hand is lost in his, it's true, and yet...

MADELAINE: He's a very pretty boy all the same.

CASTI-PIANI: (*Walking up, to* MADELAINE.) So tell me, chère belle, how is it you never let us meet your charming little princess till this evening?

MADELAINE: You find her so charming then, Marquis?

CASTI-PIANI: Absolutely adorable.

PUNTSCHUH: (*Coming toward them.*) How old is she, Cast-Piani?

CASTI-PIANI: Old enough to seem a young Queen, my dear Puntschuh.

MADELAINE: She's not quite thirteen.

PUNTSCHUH: Oh, Madame!

CASTI-PIANI: You could take her for seventeen, she is...ripe.

MADELAINE: Her father was a superb specimen, really someone, a hero!

HEILMANN: (*Coming toward them.*) With a mother as beautiful and gracious as you, Madame, it could hardly be otherwise.

PUNTSCHUH: And why have you been keeping her prisoner all this time?

MADELAINE: From maternal jealousy. She was in her convent. She's in Paris now for a mere twenty-four hours. Tomorrow evening she will return.

KADÉGA: (*Coming toward them.*) You were saying, mother dear?

MADELAINE: I was just telling these gentlemen, my treasure, that you came first in geometry.

HEILMANN: How pretty her hair is!

CASTI-PIANI: And the way she walks. This girl has breeding.

PUNTSCHUH: Her eyes bother me, I can't quite figure why.

MADELAINE: Have pity, Messieurs, she is but a child. (*Kissing* KADÉGA.) Isn't that so, little flower?

HEILMANN: You're not going to make a nun of her, are you?

MADELAINE: Of course not. But what monsters you all are! Just think, good heavens, she is still so fragile!

PUNTSCHUH: (*Walking right, and jingling the money in his pocket.*) But *this* would not bother me.

CASTI-PIANI: Seriously, Madame, you are over-doing it.

PUNTSCHUH: (*Returning.*) As for me, I'd pay you fifty Louis, believe me, if you'd let me introduce Mamzelle into the Mysteries of our particular Evangel.

MADELAINE: Well, Monsieur, I wouldn't agree to that for a million. I won't have her childhood spoiled as mine was.

CASTI-PIANI: Mamzelle won't thank you for it. Would you consent, Madame, in return for a small set of real diamonds?

MADELAINE: Blague, blague! Not all your diamonds can buy me *or* my daughter: put that in your pipe.

LUDMILLA: (*Stage right, is having a conversation with* GESCHWITZ.) Paris art schools are all good, you know, why else are we in Paris? —I'd recommend The Julian. As you enter Panorama Passage, first side street left, The Julian School.

GESCHWITZ: Dunno yet if I'll go to school, it takes so much time away from...

BIANETTA: (*Coming toward them.*) No gaming this evening?

LUDMILLA: Oh yes, Madame, we'll be playing, I only hope that...

BIANETTA: Then let's take our places, I wanna win.

GESCHWITZ: Just one moment, Mesdames, I must have a word with my petite amie.

CASTI-PIANI: (*Offering* BIANETTA *his arm.*) Madame?

BIANETTA: (*Taking it.*) Monsieur!

CASTI-PIANI: Allow me to be your other half, Madame: you have a lucky hand after all. (*He escorts her into the gaming room. Ludmilla follows.*)

MADELAINE: And, d'you have any left—of those shares in—what was that Company called again?

PUNTSCHUH: The Virgin Funicular Railway Company. I have a few thousand, but I'm holding on to them. There'll never be such a chance again.

HEILMANN: I have just one share in that Company. I wanna buy more!

PUNTSCHUH: I'll try to get you some, but you'll pay an exorbitant price.

MADELAINE: I'm lucky. I got into this business early, invested *all* my resources. (*To* PUNTSCHUH.) If unsuccessfully—you better look out!

PUNTSCHUH: One day, Madame, you'll kiss my hands. You'll make a little pilgrimage to Switzerland with Mamzelle and, climbing the mountain on this very Funicular, you'll ask God's blessing on that fertile soil, not to mention your old friend, source of all your wealth.

ALVA: You've nothing to fear, Madame, be easy. I've invested all I have—down to the last sou. I paid a high price but I don't regret it. The shares go higher every day, it's amazing.

MADELAINE: Well, so much the better. (*Taking his arm.*) Let's play. (MADELAINE, ALVA, PUNTSCHUH, LULU, HEILMANN *and* KADÉGA *go into the gaming room.* ARMANDE *and* BOB *exit on the left.*)

SCENE TWO. Rodrigo. Geschwitz.

RODRIGO: (*Back left, scribbles something on paper, folds it and holds it in his hand, noticing* GESCHWITZ.) Oh, good. —Hm. —Your grace!

GESCHWITZ: (*Down, right, winces.*)

RODRIGO: Do I look so dangerous?

GESCHWITZ: (*Looks absentmindedly at the floor.*)

RODRIGO: Your grace is not sure of the connexion?

GESCHWITZ: (*Throws a despairing glance at the center door.*)

RODRIGO: (*To himself.*) I must lighten up, make a joke. (*To her.*) May I come right out and—

GESCHWITZ: (*Utters a scream.*)

SCENE THREE. Rodrigo. Geschwitz. Casti-Piani. Lulu.

CASTI-PIANI: (*Bringing* LULU *forward from the gaming room.*) I want to have a word with you.

LULU: Please do.

RODRIGO: (*Presses the paper he'd written on into* LULU's *hand without* CASTI-PIANI *noticing, then exits to the gaming room.*)

CASTI-PIANI: And please be seated. (*To* GESCHWITZ.) Leave us alone.

GESCHWITZ: (*Does not move.*)

LULU: (*Sitting on the sofa.*) Have I annoyed you?

CASTI-PIANI: (*To* GESCHWITZ.) Are you deaf?

GESCHWITZ: (*Gives him a furious look and goes into the gaming room.*)

LULU: You feel insulted?

CASTI-PIANI: (*Sitting opposite.*) You're not insensitive, are you?

LULU: You can ask anything of me.

CASTI-PIANI: What do you have left?

LULU: You are frightful.

CASTI-PIANI: Your heart is mine already.

LULU: True. My heart is stronger than I am. I can only be thankful if you show some mercy now—

CASTI-PIANI: You make me envious—

LULU: What is it you want?

CASTI-PIANI: Count yourself fortunate that—

LULU: That it was to you I came? What can I say? You're right.

CASTI-PIANI: It's not a matter of me.

LULU: I'd never have imagined that—

CASTI-PIANI: It's a matter of the...feeling which we never permitted ourselves to...

LULU: You should thank God for that.

CASTI-PIANI: It's a bitter thing—especially if one came into this world with a heart somewhat prone to...

LULU: I'd give half my life never to have set eyes on you.

CASTI-PIANI: In the struggle for existence, one's heart takes second place.

LULU: You don't have a heart.

CASTI-PIANI: On the contrary.

LULU: Hypocrite.

CASTI-PIANI: It's my Achilles heel. Especially since I have no power over women.

LULU: Merciful God.

CASTI-PIANI: You followed your inclination and threw yourself at my feet, or I would never have known those...heavenly ecstasies...

LULU: Well may you mock me now.

CASTI-PIANI: Or the murderous torment that ensues—if one is not to get stuck indefinitely. —A model husband gone to the Devil, that's me!

LULU: Why are you telling me all this?

CASTI-PIANI: I'm Jesus in Gethsemane right now. —Financial straits. —Will God suffer this cup to pass from me?

LULU: Financial straits?

CASTI-PIANI: Murder! Help!

LULU: You are a...

CASTI-PIANI: All right, all right—

LULU: Police spy.

CASTI-PIANI: All right. I started out in the Hussars: The officers' corps.

LULU: Almighty God.

CASTI-PIANI: It was not for me. I don't want to get myself shot for other people's amusement.

LULU: You're a police spy.

CASTI-PIANI: After turning in my officer's sword, I founded an employment bureau.

LULU: Do I care?

CASTI-PIANI: I found people jobs in Hungary—Siberia, India, Persia, America...

LULU: What kind of jobs?

CASTI-PIANI: Well paid. At least for me. Till one day a preacher's wife got, so to speak, between my legs.

LULU: O God, O God.

CASTI-PIANI: Her daughter Anna, or was it Hannah, was living it up something terrible. That was blamed on me, and I was...taken over by the State.

LULU: In a penitentiary.

CASTI-PIANI: To be blunt. —After six months—thanks to my exemplary conduct and extensive command of languages— my prison door sprang open. At this point I was persuaded to settle here and keep an eye on our German countrymen when they visit Paris.

LULU: As a police spy...

CASTI-PIANI:...and to revive my employment bureau. I have the best contacts imaginable, and this is the place for it. Parisian women love Paris, especially when they're poor. The constant influx of foreigners provides abundant material.

LULU: You're laughing at me.

CASTI-PIANI: (*Taking an already opened letter from his pocket.*) I have here an offer from Epaminondas Oikonomopulos. For a "house" in Cairo. I sent them your pictures.

LULU: Which *I* gave you?

CASTI-PIANI: The one in the elf costume. The one as Pierrot. The one in the pleated blouse—and the one where you are Eve Standing Before a Mirror...

LULU: I should have realized...

CASTI-PIANI: What am I to do with it? (*Giving her the letter.*) Read this.

LULU: It's in English.

CASTI-PIANI: 600 pounds, that's 15,000 francs, 12,000 Marks...

LULU: I *can't* read it.

CASTI-PIANI: I have to guarantee that you speak French. — English you'll learn fast enough...

LULU: I can't read it.

CASTI-PIANI: (*Taking the letter back.*) Just so you see I'm no deceiver.

LULU: You are a horror.

CASTI-PIANI: I don't enjoy it. —My advice is: go. I've written these people that you're good at your work. Experienced. You are absolutely safe there.

LULU: I dunno. I don't understand.

CASTI-PIANI: I'll help you. If I take you by the throat, this minute, and hold you till the cops come, I'll have earned my 3000 Thaler.

LULU: You can't do that.

CASTI-PIANI: 4000 francs less than Epaminondas Oikonomopulos is offering for you.

LULU: Just promise you won't turn me in, then take, from my holdings, more than your Oi—Oi—

CASTI-PIANI: You have no more holdings.

LULU: I'm telling you that—

CASTI-PIANI: You've already given me everything.

LULU: I have not.

CASTI-PIANI: Everything but your Jungfrau shares.

LULU: Which are going up and up. —You can sell them.

CASTI-PIANI: I don't deal in shares. Epaminondas Oikonomopulos pays in British gold and the family of your so suddenly deceased husband pays in—

LULU: Give me time. *I'll sell them.*

CASTI-PIANI: You'll have to hurry.

LULU: Give me three days.

CASTI-PIANI: Not even one night. I'm the only one up to now that knows this rather valuable secret. You won't talk about it...

LULU: How'd you know? —Proofs...

CASTI-PIANI: That's not my affair. I've given the government attorneys to understand I'm on your trail and you've probably fled to America.

LULU: America...

CASTI-PIANI: So my advice is: let us take you to Cairo. The Epaminondas Oikonomopulos House will relieve you of all embarrassments, it's better protection than a convent.

LULU: A bordello.

CASTI-PIANI: Ever heard of a girl being taken out of a bordello to have her head chopped off? One of your customers maybe.

LULU: I won't go into a bordello. I'd rather die.

CASTI-PIANI: It's where you belong.

LULU: God help me.

CASTI-PIANI: Don't miss this chance—you'll end up on the streets.

LULU: That is not true.

CASTI-PIANI: Because you will meet with a, so to say, capital punishment.

LULU: Heavens, heavens!

CASTI-PIANI: The world over, you won't find a more glorious House, its clientele more fashionable than even Paris can offer you—Scotch Lords, Indian Governors, high Russian Officials, our own rich manufacturers from the Rhine...

LULU: Ugh!

CASTI-PIANI: You're dressed in delicate taste. You stroll around on carpets as thick as a fist. You have a fairy tale room-of-your-own with a fine view of the minarets of the El Azhar Mosque. You'll be your own woman. A lady. Supper in your own room. One won't find this anywhere in Europe.

LULU: Ugh, ugh.

CASTI-PIANI: Four weeks ago I brought in an eighteen year old girl from Berlin, a beauty from the highest aristocracy, married six months before. If you don't believe me...(*He shows her an opened letter.*) The lady does it for the fun of the thing. The husband put a bullet through his head.

LULU: (*Mechanically unfolding the paper.*) Do it for anyone that pays at the box office?

CASTI-PIANI: Look at the stamp on the envelope if you're wondering if *I* wrote it...

LULU: (*The open letter in her hand.*) My dear sir...it's just a jumble of words...

CASTI-PIANI: Her handwriting's a bit irregular. (*Takes the letter back and reads.*) "Dear Herr Gross"—that's my name—(LULU *again says: ugh.*) "When next you're in Berlin, go straight to the Conservatory and ask for Fraülein von Falati—she'll amaze you—give her the enclosed letter. Happily she's poor as a church mouse and lives with her mother in one long quarrel. I've spoken already with the Madam. Another German would be welcome if she has a good education. The Madam wants to speak with Herr Leonidas. Tell her a bit about the life here and anyway ask for a safe address where I can reach her. I've already "enthused" over things but haven't found the right words, I'm too scatterbrained. Get her stirred up, she's more beautiful than me, specially her body. Maybe she'll be more responsive to *your* efforts. She often said better Joy Supernal for eight days than a lifetime like *this*. She may be running scared, she was a virgin, but loads of temperament, don't let go of her, I pity her so much, she probably won't even marry. For me, life begins here. Everything earlier was stupid. Boring. And she has a terrific voice, which will add to the joys. I feel I arrived last evening, the time flies so fast. Tell Albert that if you see him. And he should re-marry, et cetera"—she doesn't know he's dead.

LULU: I'd rather you tore my skin off.

CASTI-PIANI: The choice is yours.

LULU: These are kids. Empty shells. —*My* days as a wild beast are over.

CASTI-PIANI: Such things return.

LULU: I could think that way when I was fifteen.

CASTI-PIANI: Sex *is* what it is, in Chinese, in Japanese—and you won't have to deal with any spiritual degradation whatsoever—You pluck the flower, and then, Good night.

LULU: I'd go crazy. —I only have myself. Can I offer my body to the first shabby character that happens along?

CASTI-PIANI: No shabby characters come *there.*

LULU: The first one, hairy as an Orangutan, the second with stinking breath, ugh! Is that what I've kept myself so clean for?

CASTI-PIANI: In the darker hours, to comfort you, there's liquor.

LULU: You're a devil.

CASTI-PIANI: How would *I* have ended up, had I let my clients' "noble rage" affect me in any way?

LULU: But why must you sell *me,* why? Look: take me anywhere you want. I am yours.

CASTI-PIANI: I have a wife and children.

LULU: You're married?!

CASTI-PIANI: At ten o' clock last night, as I was leaving a tobacco store, a young girl spoke to me—

LULU: You're NOT married?

CASTI-PIANI: It was my daughter. (*A pause. She stares fixedly at him.*) You can sacrifice yourself on silken pillows—

LULU: Only to croak in hospital—

CASTI-PIANI: Or on the executioner's block.

LULU: On...what?

CASTI-PIANI: I'd prefer the pillows.

LULU: You can't do this.

CASTI-PIANI: I'm losing 4000 francs.

LULU: It's MY head that gets cut off, my body that gets dissected.

CASTI-PIANI: I can do anything.

LULU: You are not human.

CASTI-PIANI: Thank God for that! In the time that remains, think it over. I would get you into safety before this day is out. — The police are within call. (*He goes into the gaming room, leaving the door open behind him.*)

SCENE FOUR. Lulu. After a moment Alva.

LULU: (*Motionless, she stares into space and crumples up* RODRIGO*'s note which she has held throughout the previous scene.*)

ALVA: (*Rising from behind the gaming table with a single share in his hand and coming forward to speak to* LULU.) Splendid, everything going splendidly! —Countess Geschwitz is betting her shirt! As for me, I've captured Puntschuh's last share. —Ludmilla Steinherz is making quite a bit. (*He exits down right.*)

LULU: (*Alone.*) You can't do this. (*She notices the paper in her hand, smooths it out on her knee, deciphers the content, and bursts out laughing.*)

ALVA: (*On the left, re-enters, this time with several papers in his hand.*) Aren't you joining in?

LULU: Oh, why not? (*She gets up and follows him toward the gaming room.*)

SCENE FIVE. Lulu. Geschwitz.

GESCHWITZ: (*Meeting* LULU *in the doorway.*) You're going because I'm coming.

LULU: I didn't see you.

GESCHWITZ: No, no—

LULU: God is my witness.

GESCHWITZ: (*Closing the door in the middle and coming forward.*) I have as much luck gambling as loving.

LULU: Oh, but you're lucky.

GESCHWITZ: You're mocking me.

LULU: No, you're all the rage.

GESCHWITZ: I could shoot myself.

LULU: Why not enjoy what's offered to you?

GESCHWITZ: You multiply my sufferings.

LULU: The guys turn from me to you.

GESCHWITZ: Mercy!

LULU: Spare yourself. —That poor guy is at his wits' end.

GESCHWITZ: That's how I am.

LULU: He implores me to build him up in your eyes.

GESCHWITZ: I don't even know who you're talking about.

LULU: He never leaves your side.

GESCHWITZ: Rodrigo Quast?

LULU: He's gonna jump in the Seine.

GESCHWITZ: Oh, my misery!

LULU: He's an acrobat.

GESCHWITZ: But I wouldn't exchange it for your...heartlessness.

LULU: Nor would I change places with you. Even to save my life.

GESCHWITZ: You're *taking* your life and choosing the most degrading, most disgusting way—

LULU: YOU have the gall to—?

GESCHWITZ: What's your thing with this Casti-Piani?

LULU: Silence!

GESCHWITZ: A mean specimen of manhood.

LULU: Silence!

GESCHWITZ: It's all written on his face.

LULU: Silence!

GESCHWITZ: The most bestial physiognomy I've ever set eyes on.

LULU: (*Descending on her with flashing eyes.*) Silence or I'll—

GESCHWITZ: Or you'll hit me! (*As* LULU *steps back.*) You don't even want *that*.

LULU: Not if it's you I hit.

GESCHWITZ: Listen, please, please, if you don't wish to annihilate me I gave up everything—everything—so please, please— tell me you're through with him—

LULU: And served up for you?

GESCHWITZ: (*Sliding to the floor.*) My beloved, my angel—!

LULU: God forbid: There's enough horror in my life.

GESCHWITZ: So walk on me.

LULU: Stand up, or I'll scream.

GESCHWITZ: Trample me under foot.

LULU: Stand up, or I'll call out!

GESCHWITZ: Trample on me, and then goodbye.

LULU: I won't touch you. Even with my foot.

GESCHWITZ: Trample on me. Have mercy!

LULU: I'm gonna open the doors.

GESCHWITZ: Trample me down, strangle me!

LULU: Oh, go the Moulin Rouge, go to the Café Americain!

GESCHWITZ: My love! My life!

LULU: You have money, tell Bianetta Gazil.

GESCHWITZ: You! You!

LULU: There is no end to her depravity.

GESCHWITZ: One night...

LULU: She's a woman. Like me. She has everything I have. And more, you can see that.

GESCHWITZ: One night. And then: come, death!

LULU: And of course she stays within bounds. Just as I do.

GESCHWITZ: One...night...

LULU: Not for a million.

GESCHWITZ: Lulu...(*Noise from the gaming room.*)

LULU: Stand up for God's sake.

GESCHWITZ: (*Getting up.*) I'm so miserable...

SCENE SIX. Bianetta. Madelaine. Kadéga. Ludmilla. Rodrigo. Casti-Piani. Puntschuh. Geschwitz. Heilmann. Alva.

All come from the gaming room.

LULU: (*Anxiously to* ALVA.) Is something wrong?

PUNTSCHUH: What do you think, Madame? Certainly not!

ALVA: Everyone's going for refreshments, aren't you?

MADELAINE: Everybody won, it's too thrilling!

BIANETTA: I won at least forty louis.

LUDMILLA: It's wrong to boast.

MADELAINE: That's true, it doesn't bring happiness.

BIANETTA: Even the bank won.

LUDMILLA: Not possible.

MADELAINE: It's enchanting!

ALVA: (*To* LULU.) It's really spooky—how the money keeps coming!

CASTI-PIANI: But good that it does, one needn't go without champagne.

HEILMANN: As for me, I now have enough to pay for a dinner Chez Véfour.

BIANETTA: Will you take us with you, Monsieur?

ALVA: Mesdames! To the buffet!

(*All except* RODRIGO *and* LULU *exit upstage left.*)

SCENE SEVEN. Rodrigo. Lulu.

At the door, RODRIGO *turns and comes downstage to* LULU.

RODRIGO: You read my little note?

LULU: What brought you to this absolutely shameless—

RODRIGO: Let me explain.

LULU: I don't have any 50,000 francs.

RODRIGO: Let me explain.

LULU: I have nothing now.

RODRIGO: You have three times that amount.

LULU: Even if I did...

RODRIGO: I won't let myself be intimidated.

LULU: You are shameless.

RODRIGO: But if my name was Casti-Piani....

LULU: If your name was Vasco da Gama!

RODRIGO: Why throw everything in the maw of these wild

beasts?

LULU: Everything? I have nothing.

RODRIGO: You're rolling in gold.

LULU: Almighty God!

RODRIGO: I was just talking with Monsieur le Comte...

LULU: Monsieur le Comte?

RODRIGO: Alva Schoning.

LULU: Then address yourself to him.

RODRIGO: He wouldn't give me a button. You know that.

LULU: Such a sucker, it makes your head spin.

RODRIGO: Have him give you the 50,000 francs.

LULU: You are shameless!

RODRIGO: He can refuse you nothing.

LULU: Tactless, too!

RODRIGO: He loves you so desperately.

LULU: So betray me!

RODRIGO: It would cost you one night.

LULU: Betray me.

RODRIGO: He loves you even more hotly than before. —He confided in me—he...

LULU: I should let him love me—

RODRIGO: Give up one night.

LULU: And then rob him?

RODRIGO: He would give a bundle for it.

LULU: I cannot.

RODRIGO: When I ask you?

LULU: He makes me feel sick.

RODRIGO: He's your husband after all.

LULU: Turn me in to the police. Betray me. Whether *you* do it or someone else—

RODRIGO: Don't take it so tragically. Threatening to denounce you—I wrote that just to be clear. If you were to hear my reasons—

LULU: I don't have 50,000 francs left.

RODRIGO: I need that amount, and not a centime less.

LULU: Then go ahead and betray me.

RODRIGO: What I wish to do is, um—

LULU: Yes?

RODRIGO: Are you ready?

LULU: Shoot yourself?

RODRIGO: Get myself married. To—*now* are you ready?

LULU: To Geschwitz?

RODRIGO: What?

LULU: I don't give a damn one way or the other.

RODRIGO: To an usherette at the Folies Bergère. You weren't ready for *that*.

LULU: Marry the Queen of Spain for all *I* care.

RODRIGO: I was a guest artist with the Folies Bergère. Expecting a 3000 franc engagement, but Paris doesn't appreciate me. If only I'd been a kangaroo I'd have had my picture in all the papers. Still, I made the acquaintance of Célestine Rabeux, an angel in every sense of that word. In the thirty years that she presided over the lavatory at the Folies Bergère she piled up 75,000 francs, and she'll take *me* on tomorrow—provided I contribute another 50,000. I told her I could probably get'em. She would like to withdraw from public life. And if she bade me kill my own father, I'd do it—In short we're a couple of innocent children.

LULU: Then why upset the unhappy Geschwitz with your amorous attentions?

RODRIGO: To show these Parisians a little savoir vivre.

LULU: You are a—

RODRIGO: One must do that sort of thing.

LULU: You break all promises.

RODRIGO: I regret that—

LULU: Just to meet you is to get betrayed deep down in one's soul.

RODRIGO: I got fed up with my artistic career. My strong man act yielded one disappointment after another. For me—and for the weaker sex. These girls tear the clothes off a man's body, but next thing you know, they're waltzing around with the chamber maid, and you're left sorting out their dirty linen. God help us men! —My Célestine loves me for my self alone.

LULU: I wouldn't want to come between you and your modest bride.

RODRIGO: Just give up one night.

LULU: If I envy her anything, it's her cool blood.

RODRIGO: Her ideals are not...those of a virgin.

LULU: Thank heaven for that.

RODRIGO: She knows you can't measure a husband by his John Thomas.

LULU: But if you love each other—

RODRIGO: And if you got money...

LULU: I still don't know if I *can* get you your 50,000 francs.

RODRIGO: Show him tenderness, and don't bother so much about your own pleasure.

LULU: For your sake?

RODRIGO: You can't believe how grateful I am to—

LULU: Oh, please.

RODRIGO: Making four people happy with a single stroke!

LULU: Except for me.

RODRIGO: Two men and two women—a young bridal pair among them—you still love me—a little bit?

LULU: Are you coming to lunch tomorrow?

RODRIGO: Vous êtes charmante! (*Offering his arm.*) Permettez moi, Madame la Comtesse.

LULU: (*Taking his arm.*) One loves you—a little bit—parce que *vous* êtes charmant aussi. (*Both walk left at the back.* HEILMANN *meets them in the doorway.*)

SCENE EIGHT. Lulu. Rodrigo. Heilmann. Then Puntschuh.

LULU: (*To* HEILMANN.) Are you looking for Bianetta?

HEILMANN: I'm looking for, um—

RODRIGO: (*Pointing.*) Second door on the right, sir.

LULU: A line from your Folies Bergère act? (*Both exit at left.*)

HEILMANN: (*Bumping into* PUNTSCHUH *in the doorway.*) Excuse me.

PUNTSCHUH: (*Pointing left.*) Mademoiselle Bianetta awaits you in the buffet.

HEILMANN: She wants a tête à tête with you, would you be so kind?
(*Hurries off on the right.*)

SCENE NINE. Puntschuh. Then Armande. Then Bob. Then Kadéga.

PUNTSCHUH: A tête à tête with me, eh? (*Throwing himself down in an armchair.*) Something to look forward to.

ARMANDE: (*Entering from back left heads for the gaming room.*)

PUNTSCHUH: Mademoiselle—

ARMANDE: Monsieur?

PUNTSCHUH: Bring me some sherbet, would you please?

ARMANDE: Sherbet, Monsieur. (*And she exits at the back on the right.*)

PUNTSCHUH: My God, what heat!

ARMANDE: (*Comes back with sherbet and places it on the small table beside* PUNTSCHUH.)

PUNTSCHUH: Mille fois merci, mon ange.

ARMANDE: (*Goes off into the gaming room.*)

PUNTSCHUH: Must always squeeze through—between Scylla and Charybdis! —If I don't cut *your* ears off, you'll cut mine. Must be armored—against Jews, Christians—and Syrens! My smile yields no interest, my Penis Erectus no rent: must do business with my head! My mind will not become wrinkled, will not get infected, will never need washing in Eau de Cologne, can never conceive a child, can at most conceive a speculation.

BOB: (*From behind on the left, bringing over a telegram on a tray.*) Pour Monsieur Puntschuh.

PUNTSCHUH: (*Opening the telegram and murmuring.*) ACTIONS FUNICULAIRES TOMBÉES! Virgin Funicular stock fallen! (*Pockets the telegram.*) A small fortune lost. No matter. I withheld most of my money.

BOB: No answer, Monsieur?

PUNTSCHUH: Non. Attends. (*He gives him a tip.*) What's your name?

BOB: Gaston Tarnaud, Monsieur.

PUNTSCHUH: But what do they call you hereabouts?

BOB: Bob. It's shorter.

PUNTSCHUH: Born here in Paris?

BOB: Oui, Monsieur.

PUNTSCHUH: How old are you?

BOB: Fifteen, Monsieur.*

KADÉGA: (*Entering, right.*) Maman's not here?

PUNTSCHUH: Non, ma petite. (*To himself.*) Charming girl!

KADÉGA: I can't find her, I've looked everywhere.

PUNTSCHUH: Wait, maman will be back, don't worry. —God knows, she is...(*Looking at* BOB.) And him. Those leather pants! One really doesn't know but what—God in Heaven! Shall one pluck the apple from the tree? (*Looking at* KADÉGA.) Shall one purchase the Rose of Innocence in the very Garden of Semiramis? Shall one? Or not? The little lamb stares at me: baa, baa! The little lamb's first wool! How nice it would be to change places and become delicate as a rose, slender as a sapling, chaste as a little lamb! Scary! (*He shudders and walks unsteadily between them and off at the back on the right.*)

---

* Bob's age is given as 14 at the head of the Act. He may wish Puntschuh to consider him more mature. Or Wedekind may not have been certain whether to make Bob 14 or 15.

SCENE TEN. Bob. Kadéga.

KADÉGA: (*Right.*) You haven't seen Madame Madelaine?
BOB: (*Left.*) Non, Mademoiselle.
KADÉGA: I'm so scared.
BOB: Madame must have gone up...
KADÉGA: Where?
BOB: To the third floor.
KADÉGA: What's on the third floor?
BOB: You'll find out.
KADÉGA: Tell me.
BOB: We'll hide on the stairs.
KADÉGA: Why?
BOB: Come.
KADÉGA: I'll get a scolding...
BOB: I'll show you something.
KADÉGA: What?
BOB: Come.
KADÉGA: I don't care.
BOB: You don't wanna see...
KADÉGA: Show me.
BOB: Not here!
KADÉGA: Why not?
BOB: On the third floor.
KADÉGA: I'm not going.
BOB: All right.
KADÉGA: Tell me!
BOB: Après vous, Mamzelle.
KADÉGA: Non!
BOB: Mais oui!

SCENE ELEVEN. Madelaine. Bob. Kadéga.

MADELAINE: (*From the back, left, in unspeakable excitement.*) Oú

est-elle donc? Ah, here she is, my God! (*Pulling her around.*)
Que fais-tu là? Aren't you ashamed, you bad girl, hein?

KADÉGA: (*Breaks out in tears.*) Oh, maman, I was looking for
you.

MADELAINE: Looking for me, looking for me, did I tell you to
look for me?

KADÉGA: Oh, maman, maman!

MADELAINE: Liar. What were you up to with this boy? Tell me,
please tell me...

KADÉGA: I was looking for you, maman.

MADELAINE: Oh là là! You would see me soon enough! I didn't
bring you here to make eyes at the groom. —No, no, be
quiet. —You scared me so.

SCENE TWELVE. Alva. Rodrigo. Heilmann. Bianetta. Ludmilla. Puntschuh. Geschwitz. Lulu. and Casti-Piani. (from the back on the right). The foregoing.

BOB: (*Knocks down a half glass of champagne that was on the table
and hurries back left.*)

MADELAINE: (*Drying* KADÉGA's *eyes.*) Don't cry, you know.

LULU: (*On* CASTI-PIANI's *arm, to* KADÉGA.) What's up, child, what
are you crying for?

PUNTSCHUH: You've been crying, Mademoiselle?

LUDMILLA: Poor little thing.

BIANETTA: (*To* KADÉGA.) What is bothering you? Tell me.

PUNTSCHUH: Reminds one of that romance of teen-age
innocence...?

HEILMANN: Paul and Virginia?* Virginia—Kadéga—so pretty

---

* In Bernadin de St. Pierre's novel of that name. Bob and Kadéga are a
grotesque mirror-image (image in a distorting mirror) of that teenage couple
brought up in a "state of nature" far from corrupting "civilization." Paul and
Virginia ends with the shipwrecked Virginia choosing to drown rather than
remove her clothes in order to let an unclothed sailor take her on his back and
swim ashore.

with tears in her eyes?

MADELAINE: It's her nerves. It's too soon for that sort of thing. Can we change the subject?

PUNTSCHUH: You are too severe, Madame, she's at the most difficult age, you'll give her anemia.

GESCHWITZ: I'd be just as happy back at the gaming table.

RODRIGO: (*Offering his arm.*) Your Grace...

GESCHWITZ: Go to hell.

RODRIGO: Wow! You'll pay for this. (*They all go into the gaming room except for* LULU *and* CASTI-PIANI.)

CASTI-PIANI: Make your decision by the time I bid you good night.

LULU: You cannot do it.

CASTI-PIANI: What were you talking about just now—with that former lover of yours?

LULU: Who?

CASTI-PIANI: The high jumper.

LULU: Secrets of love.

CASTI-PIANI: You will pay with your head.

LULU: You can NOT do it. (*They start to join the others in the gaming room.* BOB, *entering upstage left, stops* LULU *in the doorway and whispers something to her.*)

LULU: Let him in. (*To* CASTI-PIANI.) Excuse me. Two minutes.

CASTI-PIANI: I can do anything. (*Exits to the gaming room.*)

SCENE THIRTEEN. Lulu. Bob. Schigolch.

BOB: (*Back left.*) Monsieur!

SCHIGOLCH: (*Entering and giving* BOB *a look.*) Holy smokes!

LULU: My groom.

SCHIGOLCH: Where d'you find *him*?

LULU: At the Fernando Circus.

SCHIGOLCH: What can he do?

LULU: Dress horses.

SCHIGOLCH: What's he doing here?

LULU: Learning things.

SCHIGOLCH: How much does he get an hour?

LULU: Ask him.

SCHIGOLCH: I don't have enough French.

LULU: He gets four and twenty on his bare behind.

SCHIGOLCH: With what implement?

LULU: (*To* BOB.) Close the doors.

SCHIGOLCH: (*Following him with his eyes.*) He's broader than you.

LULU: (*Shaking her head.*) With my two hands...(*Implied is: "I spank him.".*)

SCHIGOLCH: (*To* BOB *who is closing the doors.*) You can be on your way.

LULU: Our hip measurements are the same.

SCHIGOLCH: (*To* BOB.) It's a pretty good situation for you here?

BOB: Mais oui, Monsieur, Madame is so beautiful—and so good.

LULU: You can bring us a small Chartreuse.

BOB: Avec plaisir, Madame. (*He exits on the right.*)

SCENE FOURTEEN. Schigolch. Lulu.

SCHIGOLCH: (*Sinking into an armchair.*) I need 500 francs, I've got to furnish an apartment for my girlfriend, she wants her very own furniture.

LULU: Good Heavens, you still have a girlfriend?

SCHIGOLCH: With God's help.

LULU: You and your eighty years?

SCHIGOLCH: Why else are we in Paris?

LULU: God.

SCHIGOLCH: She wasn't born yesterday either.

LULU: Heavens.

SCHIGOLCH: In our damn Germany I've lived too long in holes and corners.

LULU: God have mercy!

SCHIGOLCH: You haven't seen me in six weeks.

LULU: I can't take it any more, it is simply too, too...

SCHIGOLCH: Too, too?

LULU: (*Collapses, buries her head between his knees, and shakes with convulsive sobbing.*) Too...too...hideous.

SCHIGOLCH: I was in the, um, clink the whole time. (*Stroking her hair.*) You take it too hard, you must have a couple days off.

LULU: What have I done to deserve it? What have I done, God in Heaven? I can't go through with it.

SCHIGOLCH: Got out yesterday. (*Stroking her.*) You must wash yourself with snow. —Scream if it will do you any good...

LULU: (*Groaning.*) Oh God, God.

SCHIGOLCH: I learnt French in there. —You must take salt baths. —Scream! Let it out! —Take a French novel to bed with you once a week.

LULU: What will become of me?

SCHIGOLCH: It will soon be over. Have a good cry. I had you on my knee like this. Good God, it's nearly twenty years ago. How time passes. When you were growing up, you screamed the same way. —I know you inside out, huh? —I stroked your hair and rubbed your knees till they were warm. You didn't have a white satin dress then—no feathers in your hair—no see-through stockings. —You had NO stockings, hardly even a shirt. But you had that scream even then!

LULU: Take me with you. Please! Take pity on me! Take me back. Right now. Take me to your attic.

SCHIGOLCH: Me? Take YOU with me?

LULU: In your attic, your attic.

SCHIGOLCH: And my...500 francs?

LULU: Oh, God.

SCHIGOLCH: You carry on—beyond your powers. Give your body the time it needs to quiet down.

LULU: My life is threatened.

SCHIGOLCH: Who by?

LULU: He plans to betray me.

SCHIGOLCH: Who?

LULU: He plans to—

SCHIGOLCH: What?

LULU: Cut my head off.

SCHIGOLCH: Who plans to cut your head off? I may be eighty but—

LULU: I see myself gagged and bound.

SCHIGOLCH: Who plans to cut your head off?

LULU: Rodrigo. Rodrigo Quast.

SCHIGOLCH: Him?!

LULU: He's given me to understand as much.

SCHIGOLCH: Lose no sleep over it. —I'll take him to some restaurant and—

LULU: Do him in, please, do him in. (*Pause.*) Yeah: do him in— you can if you want to.

SCHIGOLCH: He's a wild card all right, forever saying what he knows ain't so...

LULU: Do him in.

SCHIGOLCH: Making a bit too much of himself.

LULU: For love of your own child: do him in.

SCHIGOLCH: Actually, I don't know whose child you are.

LULU: I won't stand up again till you've promised me...

SCHIGOLCH: That poor swine.

LULU: So do him in.

SCHIGOLCH: Once he's gone, you can't bring him to life again. (*Silence.*) I could throw him out of my window and into the Seine.

LULU: Please!

SCHIGOLCH: What's in it for me?

LULU: Do it.

SCHIGOLCH: What's in it for me?

LULU: 500 francs.

SCHIGOLCH: 500...500...?

LULU: Okay, 1000.

SCHIGOLCH: If I can make this my trade here in Paris—I can become a rich man...

LULU: How much d'you want?

SCHIGOLCH: And drive my own coach despite my age.

LULU: How much d'you want?

SCHIGOLCH: If *you* would just—

LULU: Me?

SCHIGOLCH: Lower your guard.

LULU: God have mercy.

SCHIGOLCH: Like it used to be.

LULU: With—you?

SCHIGOLCH: You have such lovely clothes now.

LULU: What do you want—from me?

SCHIGOLCH: You'll soon find out.

LULU: I'm not...the way I was.

SCHIGOLCH: You find me—an abomination?

LULU: You have someone.

SCHIGOLCH: Yeah, and she's sixty-five years old.

LULU: What do the two of you do?

SCHIGOLCH: Play patience.

LULU: But with me?

SCHIGOLCH: You're gonna find out.

LULU: You're a cruel man.

SCHIGOLCH: It's a long time since we knew each other.

LULU: All right then.

SCHIGOLCH: We'll refresh both our memories.

LULU: (*Getting up.*) SWEAR to me that...

SCHIGOLCH: When will you come over?

LULU: God in Heaven.

SCHIGOLCH: When I'm alone, that is.

LULU: Whenever you want.

SCHIGOLCH: In your white satin costume...

LULU: But you WILL throw him down?

SCHIGOLCH: With pearls and diamonds?

LULU: Just as I am.

SCHIGOLCH: I want to get back to debauchery!

LULU: You SWEAR?

SCHIGOLCH: Just send him over.

LULU: You swear, you swear...

SCHIGOLCH: By all that's holy!

LULU: You'll bring him down?

SCHIGOLCH: I swear.

LULU: By all that's holy?

SCHIGOLCH: (*Who is groping under the hem of her skirt.*) What
more d'you want?

LULU: (*Trembling.*) By all that's holy?

SCHIGOLCH: By all that's holy.

LULU: Good. Now I can calm down.

SCHIGOLCH: (*Letting her dress drop.*) You're on fire—with hate.
(*Pause.* LULU *walks left, straightens out her dress, adjusts her
hair in front of the mirror, and dries her tears.*)

LULU: Now go. Go.

SCHIGOLCH: It has to be today?

LULU: So that you're home when he arrives—with her.

SCHIGOLCH: Her?

LULU: (*Feeling her cheeks and powdering them.*) He'll come with
the Countess.

SCHIGOLCH: A Countess?

LULU: You're heating up some grog. You say it's the Countess'
room, you live next door. —The Countess gets drunk. —
You give him all you've got.

SCHIGOLCH: Yeah, he gets his.

LULU: If you can carry him? God. God.

SCHIGOLCH: Only three steps to the window.

LULU: In the morning the Countess will quietly slip out.

SCHIGOLCH: Even if I have to roll him over, toward that

window?

LULU: She won't know which house it was at.

SCHIGOLCH: Anyway the window's high enough up.

LULU: Remember one thing: I want his earrings.

SCHIGOLCH: When he's down, I say good bye to my four walls.

LULU: D'you hear me—his gold earrings?

SCHIGOLCH: What is it now?

LULU: My garter.

SCHIGOLCH: Why are you staring at me?

LULU: My garter's undone.

SCHIGOLCH: I'll find a room behind the Bastille. (LULU *has pulled her skirt up and is re-tying the garter.*)

SCHIGOLCH: Or behind the Buttes-Chaumont. —Yellow stockings...

LULU: Orange.

SCHIGOLCH: What an aroma!

LULU: All orange. With the white satin. (*Upright now.*) Go. Go now.

SCHIGOLCH: Orange, hm. —And who is his Countess?

LULU: That madwoman, *you* know. —You must go by coach.

SCHIGOLCH: Of course.

LULU: Who kisses my feet. Now, please go.

SCHIGOLCH: (*Leaving.*) His gold earrings. (LULU *takes him out, upstage left.*)

SCENE FIFTEEN. Casti-Piani. Rodrigo Quast.

CASTI-PIANI *pushes* RODRIGO *into the Salon by center door.*

CASTI-PIANI: (*Shaking him.*) What were you discussing with her...?

RODRIGO: Nothing, nothing.

CASTI-PIANI: (*Hitting him in the belly with his knee.*) You bastard.

RODRIGO: God.

CASTI-PIANI: You have a date?

RODRIGO: I can't get it together anymore—

CASTI-PIANI: How about a confession? (*Hits him again.*)

RODRIGO: I'm getting married, so please spare me, I AM getting married...

CASTI-PIANI: A rendez-vous?

RODRIGO: To a native, a Parisian. By all that's holy, a local woman, spare me, it's a matter of money, she has to deliver.

CASTI-PIANI: (*Drawing a revolver.*) Liar!

RODRIGO: Oh, stop, stop. Inform yourself. It all hinges on money, just money. *She* shot someone.

CASTI-PIANI: (*Lets him go and walks right.*) Then excuse me, you see I'm in love...and when I'm in love, I become—

RODRIGO: A grisly kind o' guy?

CASTI-PIANI: (*Going into the gambling room.*) Good evening.

SCENE SIXTEEN. Rodrigo.

RODRIGO: A wild character, God save us. —A guy I could throw up to the ceiling with one hand. (*Looking around, frightened.*) Nu?

SCENE SEVENTEEN. Lulu. Rodrigo.

RODRIGO: Oh you. Thank God.

LULU: Me, yes. —I come now...

RODRIGO: God reward you for it.

LULU: I come from Geschwitz.

RODRIGO: Oh yes. Yes, yes I was just telling her...

LULU: You told me too.

RODRIGO: What I said, well, I told her...

LULU: She repeated it to me.

RODRIGO: What I said, well, I told her...

LULU: That she was the first girl...

RODRIGO: Something like that.

LULU: That you've ever wanted to make love to.

RODRIGO: The first girl to stiffen my...backbone, bring out the best in me...She took all that a certain way.

LULU: She went half crazy.

RODRIGO: A matter of little concern to me.

LULU: It's the first time she ever heard the like.

RODRIGO: If only things went half so well with Célestine!

LULU: You haven't got any further with her yet?

RODRIGO: We're 50,000 francs short.

LULU: I've promised them to you.

RODRIGO: That's my girl.

LULU: On one condition.

RODRIGO: When d'you intend to...

LULU: You must make Geschwitz happy.

RODRIGO: That I can't do.

LULU: As you wish.

RODRIGO: I can't do it.

LULU: As you wish.

RODRIGO: I don't believe it'll work.

LULU: As you wish.

RODRIGO: There's nothing to wish. For me this person is an aristocrat and that's all.

LULU: You never tried the aristocracy?

RODRIGO: Many times. They fell on me like flies, princesses, duchesses—but *they* had legs, by golly.

LULU: You don't know her legs yet.

RODRIGO: And don't want to.

LULU: As you wish.

RODRIGO: I can't do it, believe me.

LULU: A he man like you.

RODRIGO: My strength's in my arms, see these biceps?

LULU: Spare me your biceps. If you don't want to, you understand what that will mean. —Now, look, she and I are friends.

RODRIGO: I meant no offense, our relationship has been Platonic. That happens among educated people: our life isn't all Ho-Yo-To-Ho.

LULU: *Our* life?

RODRIGO: Well, maybe yours *is*. Have you ever loved a human being for himself alone?

LULU: Do I just go in for bathroom sex?

RODRIGO: You're the bathroom.

LULU: (*Biting her lip.*) What can I tell the Countess?

RODRIGO: Tell her I've been castrated.

LULU: As you wish. (*She goes upstage.*)

RODRIGO: (*Turning.*) Wha—what does she want?

LULU: To be made love to.

RODRIGO: I can't even imagine it.

LULU: Rely on your stomach muscles.

RODRIGO: If I'd had any idea...

LULU: Why did you make her mouth water?

RODRIGO: Sexy as an umbrella frame.

LULU: She's still a virgin.

RODRIGO: And you are a...If a guy was hanging from the gallows, you'd stick your tongue out at him.

LULU: Not any more, I've changed.

RODRIGO: I guess I know *that.*

LULU: You found me ungrateful but...

RODRIGO: I'll do it. —I'll show *her.* what will a guy not do for love? (*He goes back right.*)

LULU: Where are you off to?

RODRIGO: First I gotta eat a caviar sandwich. (*Exit, right.*)

LULU: (*Opening the center door she calls into the gaming room.*) Martha!

SCENE EIGHTEEN. Lulu. Countess Geschwitz.

GESCHWITZ: (*Entering with downcast eyes.*) Lulu!

LULU: (*Bringing her forward.*) If you do as I say tonight—are you
  listening?

GESCHWITZ: Yes.

LULU: Listen up. —Then tomorrow night you *can.*

GESCHWITZ: Can? What?

LULU: Sleep with me.

GESCHWITZ: (*Seizes* LULU'*s hand and covers it with kisses.*) Oh!

LULU: You can undress me...and do my hair.

GESCHWITZ: Oh, Lulu

LULU: (*Freeing her hand.*) But now...

GESCHWITZ: Speak.

LULU: Now you have to go with Rodrigo.

GESCHWITZ: What for?

LULU: What for, what for?

GESCHWITZ: Yes, what on earth for?

LULU: That much you know.

GESCHWITZ: With a man?

LULU: Yes, yes, be glad of it!

GESCHWITZ: For God's sake!

LULU: With a man—that's why you're a girl.

GESCHWITZ: Ask anything of me, however frightful, anything...

LULU: *I* had to do it before I could count up to three. I wasn't
  glad of *that.*

GESCHWITZ: You can have my life if you want it, but please...

LULU: It may even cure you.

GESCHWITZ: A man...I cannot.

LULU: And a woman—*I* cannot. (GESCHWITZ *turns away, ties
  herself in knots, unties herself, clenches her firsts, breaks out in
  hysterical sobbing and, supporting herself on the mantelpiece,
  silently weeps into a handkerchief.*)

LULU: D'you think I'd let you—you! —into my bedroom if this
  man wasn't holding his axe over my head, threatening me,
  threatening to sell me? So with my body I save my head.

GESCHWITZ: (*Straightening up.*) What is it you want me to do?

LULU: He'll be here any minute.

GESCHWITZ: And then?

LULU: Storm the fortress, work on him.

GESCHWITZ: To what end?

LULU: What end, how stupid can you be?

GESCHWITZ: No, no...but...I don't know how, it's the...first time.

LULU: Act like you were in love with him.

GESCHWITZ: God forfend!

LULU: He requires that. —Or he'll go haywire.

GESCHWITZ: I'll do...what I can.

LULU: He's a he man, and you've rubbed him the wrong way.

GESCHWITZ: What if he doesn't believe me?

LULU: Get a cab at the door and tell the driver: 75 Quai de la Gare.

GESCHWITZ: Yes.

LULU: Shall I write it down?

GESCHWITZ: Yes.

LULU: (*Does the writing on the mantel, then gives* GESCHWITZ *a card.*) 75 Quai de la Gare. —When you get out, pay the driver...

GESCHWITZ: (*Taking the card.*) Yes.

LULU: That's a hotel. Tell Rodrigo you're staying there.

GESCHWITZ: Yes.

LULU: That's it. Nothing else to worry about.

GESCHWITZ: (*Shudders from head to foot.*)

LULU: He can't take you to his room, he hasn't got one, his pockets are empty. (*Opening the door upstage right, she calls out.*) Monsieur, s'il vous plaît!

SCENE NINETEEN. Rodrigo. Lulu. Geschwitz.

RODRIGO: (*Comes with his mouth full from upstage right.*)

LULU: (*Whispering in* GESCHWITZ' *ear in passing.*) Throw your arms round his neck.

RODRIGO: (*Chewing.*) Pray excuse me!

GESCHWITZ: (*Goes to* RODRIGO *with downcast eyes and hangs about his neck.*)

RODRIGO: So we're off to a fast start.

LULU: You want a coach? There are several on the street.

RODRIGO: (*Groaning, to* GESCHWITZ.) So let go of me, will you?

GESCHWITZ: (*Seeing him from under half closed eyelids.*) I love you.

RODRIGO: God protect me!

GESCHWITZ: (*Tries to take him with her.*)

RODRIGO: Who would ever have seen this in the old grey mare?

GESCHWITZ: (*Both hands before her face.*) I can't go on.

RODRIGO: (*Wringing his hands.*) Couldn't you find another way?

LULU: (*Icily, near* GESCHWITZ.) You know what hinges on this?

GESCHWITZ: (*Hands to her temples.*) O God, O God, O God!

RODRIGO: Did I ever talk dirty in your presence? Did I pinch your bottom so much as once? Tomorrow I'll bring you a machine and you can wind it up every night—ten times— which can't be done with me.

LULU: (*Close to him.*) And your 50,000 francs?

GESCHWITZ: (*With troubled eyes seizing him violently by the coat.*) Fall on me and get it done, I feel faint.

RODRIGO: (*His hand to his collar.*) Though it's true I was never so handsomely paid for this kind of thing. (*Offering her his arm.*) Let us ascend the scaffold. (*He leads her left.*)

LULU: (*Near* GESCHWITZ.) You have the card?

GESCHWITZ: It's killing me. I won't live through this.

LULU: (*Opening the door for them.*) Bonne nuit, mes enfants! (*Comes forward and sinks into a chair.*) I'm so tired. (*Pause.*)

SCENE TWENTY. Frightful noise in the gaming room. The door bursts open. Puntschuh, Heilmann, then Alva and Bianetta, Madelaine, Kadéga, and Ludmilla come into the salon. Later, Bob, then a Plainclothesman and Casti-Piani.

LULU *gets up, trembling.* HEILMANN *holds securities in his hand. The document on top has brightly colored print on it and an Alpine scene.*

HEILMANN: (*To* PUNTSCHUH.) Il vous faut l'accepter, Monsieur, you must accept it.

PUNTSCHUH: Leave me in peace.

LULU: What's the matter now?

HEILMANN: (*To* PUNTSCHUH.) D'you want me to call the police?

ALVA: (*To* HEILMANN.) Keep your trap shut.

LULU: Mon dieu!

LUDMILLA: It's these shares...

HEILMANN: (*Pointing to* PUNTSCHUH.) *He* sold them to us, him.

ALVA: Shut up.

PUNTSCHUH: That's not legal tender, not marketable, mon cher.

HEILMANN: You're refusing to give me my return. Thief! Scumbag!

BIANETTA: Les allemands, these Germans, such language!

MADELAINE: D'you understand any of this?

LUDMILLA: He's taken his money...

HEILMANN: Yeah, watch him quit, watch him leave the game, the shark.

PUNTSCHUH: Me, leaving the game? Ha!

MADELAINE: Oh, this is not nice...

PUNTSCHUH: Saying he needs assets in cash, what the hell? I'm not in my Bureau de Change here, let him come at ten in the morning, presenting his papers!

HEILMANN: Paper? (*Pointing to a share.*) This is money. This is 1600 francs, the share you sold me.

PUNTSCHUH: Not marketable, I repeat. For gaming, you need cash.

HEILMANN: Not marketable? When you're holding the bank, when you're squeezing the last sou out of someone— suddenly "not marketable"?

KADÉGA: Qu'est-ce qu'il a, maman?

MADELAINE: Je n'en sais rien, moi.

BIANETTA: On ne comprends rien.

ALVA: (*To* PUNTSCHUH.) Won't you accept the shares?

PUNTSCHUH: (*Wiping his brow.*) Like hell I will.

HEILMANN: Cutthroat! Jewish pig!

PUNTSCHUH: Mais voyons, mon ami, soyez raisonable! It has no value, your title.

HEILMANN: My share?

PUNTSCHUH: Without value, cher enfant.

ALVA: (*To* PUNTSCHUH.) Are you crazy?

HEILMANN: Without value?

MADELAINE: What's this? Our shares?

LULU: (*Bringing* PUNTSCHUH *forward.*) Explain yourself, Monsieur.

PUNTSCHUH: Our Jungfrau Funicular Shares, my friends, fell this evening, fell to fifteen.

MADELAINE: (*Sinking down with a small scream.*) Oh, my God!

KADÉGA: (*Throwing herself upon her.*) Maman, maman!

PUNTSCHUH: A misfortune, ah yes! I just got the news by telegram. At first I didn't want to pass it on.

ALVA: (*Pale as death.*) Is it possible?

LULU: Well, well, we're done for.

PUNTSCHUH: (*Taking a telegram from his breast pocket.*) Me, too, I've lost a fortune. Tomorrow, on the Bourse, they'll spell out how many centimes they'll pay on the franc.

LULU: (*Who has taken the telegram, reads it.*) "...fallen to 55, then risen to 340, fallen to 15..." (*To herself.*) To Cairo then! On to Cairo! (*Exits upstage right.*)

MADELAINE: (*Sobbing.*) Eighteen years of work...sufferings...(*She faints.*)

KADÉGA: Maman, maman! (*Puts her arm under her head.*) Wake up! She's dying, she's dying.

PUNTSCHUH: (*Withdrawing.*) If she jumps up now, she'll scratch my eyes out.

BIANETTA: Where are you off to, Monsieur?

PUNTSCHUH: I'm in a hurry...taking a coach...

BIANETTA: Will you take me to supper Chez Silvain?

PUNTSCHUH: Why?

BIANETTA: Because you've just lost a fortune.

PUNTSCHUH: Good idea. We can console each other. There's nothing left here. Chez Silvain! (*Both exit upstage left.* LULU *comes out of the gaming room followed by* BOB.)

LULU: (*Softly to* ALVA.) Have you seen Casti-Piani?

ALVA: (*Bent over* MADELAINE.) She's alive, look, she's coming to.

LULU: Have you seen Casti-Piani?

ALVA: Who?

LUDMILLA: Monsieur Casti-Piani left when the game started up again.

LULU: (*To* ALVA.) We are lost.

BOB: Monsieur took his hat and coat twenty minutes ago.

LULU: (*To* BOB.) Viens avec moi. (LULU *and* BOB *exit downstage right.*)

ALVA: (*Holding a phial under* MADELAINE*'s nose.*) She's breathing. Breathing *in*. How lovely she is, this woman! She's shivering, her hands are frozen.

KADÉGA: (*Sobbing.*) Maman, Maman!

ALVA: Now she's moving, so don't be worried, Mademoiselle.

LUDMILLA: Open her corsage a little so she can breathe more freely.

HEILMANN: (*With his share in his hands.*) That's what you get.

LUDMILLA: Why speculate on Jungfrau shares?

HEILMANN: I'd won 2,000 francs on the Grand Prix,

LUDMILLA: You could have bought a bicycle with that.

HEILMANN: That beast of prey was poised to jump. My evil genius placed me in his path.

LUDMILLA: You will now bring out some pieces in the Berlin papers and repair the damage!

HEILMANN: You can talk. I'm not as adept as you.

LUDMILLA: Tell your readers what you've seen.

HEILMANN: Would you help me with that?

LUDMILLA: Let's see now. D'you know The Dog That Smokes?

HEILMANN: No, no.

LUDMILLA: The Sheep with Five Paws?

HEILMANN: Non, ma belle.

LUDMILLA: The Suckling Calf?

HEILMANN: I don't know any of these places.

LUDMILLA: Let's go to the Sheep with Five Paws, it's next to Les Halles. We'll be at home there. By daybreak we'll have written a nice little column.

HEILMANN: You don't sleep?

LUDMILLA: At night? Never. (*Both exit upstage left.*)

KADÉGA: (*As her mother opens her eyes.*) Wake up, maman.

MADELAINE: Where am I?

ALVA: (*Helping her rise.*) Come, Madame, sit over here...

KADÉGA: Come, Maman.

MADELAINE: My child...

KADÉGA: My poor little maman, where on earth...?

MADELAINE: O my God...it was nothing...but.

KADÉGA: But...

MADELAINE: We are paupers now.

KADÉGA: Don't say that.

MADELAINE: After eighteen years, years of hard work.

KADÉGA: And what do we have to be ashamed of?

MADELAINE: To think back to youth, happy days long past!

KADÉGA: What matter? —I'm gonna earn enough money for two.

MADELAINE: (*Kissing* KADÉGA.) Thank you, my child.

KADÉGA: Say no to those thoughts. I shall never leave you.

MADELAINE: Do you know what you're saying? (LULU, *downstage right, opens the door without passing through it. She is wearing light-colored leather pants, red jacket, gleaming topboots, a dark riding cloak over her shoulders, a jockey's cap in her hand; hair cut short.*)

LULU: (*Quietly.*) Alva! Alva!

ALVA: (*Caught in* KADÉGA's *gaze at the moment turns quickly round.*) Me voilà. —Are you out of your mind?

LULU: We haven't a moment to lose.

ALVA: How so? We could easily—

LULU: (*Two steps forward.*) We've been betrayed.

ALVA: Wha—wha—what—?

LULU: *You* enter a penitentiary and *I* get my head chopped off.

ALVA: (*Down on his knees.*) Lulu...

LULU: Get that safebox, put your coat round it.

ALVA: I have—the key.

LULU: Come on, every minute counts.

ALVA: (*Stunned.*) Who is...?

LULU: What matter who? Come on.

ALVA: You let them scare you...

LULU: Casti-Piani.

ALVA: Your lover.

LULU: Come on. (*Both exit down left.*)

MADELAINE: (*Keeping* KADÉGA *at her side.*) Enfin, qu'est-ce que cela veut dire?

KADÉGA: Everyone's on the run.

MADELAINE: Like there was cholera in the house.

KADÉGA: Let's go home, maman.

MADELAINE: Yeah, and to bed. But Oh, my God, this life of ours!

KADÉGA: Don't cry, Maman, please don't cry, I don't want to go back to my convent. No, I'll work.

MADELAINE: At thirteen?

KADÉGA: Yes, yes, what does that have to do with it?

MADELAINE: God bless you!

KADÉGA: Let's see now, maman—

MADELAINE: I must try other things. Maybe an engagement at the Concert Parisien, who knows? I'm not Yvette Guilbert but I have a nice voice and a pile of costumes. I'll sing my catastrophe it'll amuse them.

KADÉGA: Don't you want to take me with you?

MADELAINE: Absolutely not.

KADÉGA: Why not, maman?

MADELAINE: In your baby skirt? What are you thinking of?

KADÉGA: Well, just that.

MADELAINE: You'll break my heart yet.

KADÉGA: They'll like me that way.

MADELAINE: Who told you that?

KADÉGA: I just know. You'll see—

MADELAINE: All right. —Right.

KADÉGA: You'll take me along?

MADELAINE: We'll go to the Olympia, tomorrow evening if you like—

KADÉGA: If I like!

MADELAINE: We'll reserve a box for the two of us.

KADÉGA: We'll be seen together in the lobby at intermission.

MADELAINE: Poor child.

KADÉGA: I'll love it.

MADELAINE: God forgive me.

KADÉGA: Take me, maman, take me there!

MADELAINE: Even so I should say a few words to you.

KADÉGA: Or you could leave them till tomorrow.

MADELAINE: With those big clear eyes of yours and that skin so fresh and sparkling!

KADÉGA: I'm not afraid.

MADELAINE: In a short time you'll be very changed.

KADÉGA: I'll do whatever you wish.

MADELAINE: And afterwards you may not feel satisfied...

KADÉGA: I'm not gonna get killed.

MADELAINE: If one could only be sure of that, my God.

KADÉGA: And you'll have something to live on. —You know, I'd be glad to die for you, maman.

MADELAINE: Baron Fouquet maybe. —He's sixty years old.

PLAINCLOTHESMAN: (*Entering from upstage left.*) In the name of the law, you are under arrest.

MADELAINE: Me?

CASTI-PIANI: (*Entering.*) No, no, no!

END OF ACT FOUR

London, 1888. LULU has slipped through CASTI-PIANI's fingers and has had RODRIGO QUAST murdered, keeping her promise to sleep with the contracted murderer, SCHIGOLCH. When the latter and her husband ALVA run out of funds, it is proposed that LULU provide for the trio by walking the streets of Whitechapel, haunted, as they were at the time, by Jack the Ripper, for whom the uterus seems to have been Pandora's box. Rumor had it that he would cut out the uterus of each of his victims and carry it off.

ACT FIVE

London. Attic. No mansard windows but just two skylights opening outwards on the sloping roof. On each side, left and right, downstage, an ill-fitting door of rough-hewn wood with primitive fittings. At the proscenium on the right, a torn gray mattress. Downstage left, a flowerstand painted red with a bottle of whisky on it. Beside the whisky bottle, a small smoky petroleum lamp. Backstage left, an old green chaise longue. On the right near the center door, a wicker chair, the seat in holes. —Walls painted reddish. Rain is heard on the roof. Downstage left, it is leaking through a hole. Water on the floor.

SCENE ONE. Schigolch. Alva. Lulu.

On a mattress to the right lies schigolch in a long gray great coat that has flaps and skirts reaching down to his feet. On the chaise longue backstage left lies ALVA SCHONING, his hands clasped behind his head, wrapped in a red rug, the strap of which is hanging on the wall above him. LULU, barefoot, her hair grown fairly long, falling loosely over her shoulders, wearing torn black clothes, enters downstage left, carrying a washbasin.

SCHIGOLCH: What are you waiting for?

ALVA: She has to get washed first.

SCHIGOLCH: They don't bother about that over here.

ALVA: She has such *noble* inclinations.

LULU: (*Placing the basin where it catches the raindrops.*) If only we could first make an end of *you.*

ALVA: She can't wait for that.

LULU: (*Straightening up and throwing her hair back.*) God knows I can't!

SCHIGOLCH: So go now, kid.

ALVA: (*Rolling over on his back.*) My wife, my wife, my wife!

LULU: But you're not worth making an end of.

SCHIGOLCH: Starting out is always troublesome. Complicated. It's like that in every business.

ALVA: That basin's overflowing.

LULU: Where'm I supposed to take it?

SCHIGOLCH: Listen! (*The rain is drumming on the roof.*) The drums are signaling roll call! This rain creates the atmosphere for your début!

LULU: (*Staggering.*) I wish I was where you can kick me and I won't wake up.

SCHIGOLCH: In another three days, ten horses won't be able to hold you back. You gotta wait and that joyful feeling just arrives! I've seen it a dozen times in my life. At the start, hell to pay. Later, you wouldn't change things for a million Marks.

ALVA: You're going on this pilgrimage barefoot?

LULU: My shoes are wet.

SCHIGOLCH: Old England won't mind.

LULU: (*To ALVA.*) Let the old man go out there, he wouldn't even have to unbutton his greatcoat.

SCHIGOLCH: In this weather? When you wouldn't turn a dog from your door?

LULU: But me you would.

SCHIGOLCH: She'd rather see us starve than have some fun.

ALVA: I don't hold it against her. Prostituting one's most intimate feelings—

SCHIGOLCH: Dumb cluck.

LULU: (*Sitting on the floor by the wall and putting her arms round her knees.*) Ooh, it's so cold.

ALVA: I dreamt we were dining Chez Silvain.

SCHIGOLCH: With your talent for languages she has a great future before her here.

ALVA: Bianetta was there. I'd ordered those horse-shoe pastries hard to scoop'em up.

LULU: I'd like to warm myself up on one of you.

ALVA: I could feel them in my stomach. —It made me cry. — The dishes rattled. —I had champagne all over my shirt, I was too drunk, it flowed right past my mouth—

SCHIGOLCH: Ah, yes!

LULU: I can't feel my hands or my feet.

SCHIGOLCH: She's wasting the rush hour—when people leave after dinner.

LULU: I'd rather freeze.

ALVA: Me too. It's a dog's life, why drag it out? End of the line.

LULU: I should stuff someone's mouth with the little bit of life I have left?

SCHIGOLCH: Come on. Get your shoes on.

ALVA: I won't touch such...tainted food.

SCHIGOLCH: She used to do it—before she knew the score.

LULU: And you drank the money away.

SCHIGOLCH: At ten years old she could have supported Father and Mother.

ALVA: (*Writhing.*) A steak, Katya! A steak, my kingdom for a...a...

SCHIGOLCH: Kick her downstairs. I can't any more, I'm too old and frail.

LULU: I'm to be on the street and never get off it? I'd have found something here long ago, if only I'd gone riding in Hyde Park one single time. But now I've nothing but rags to wear: I'm going to hell.

SCHIGOLCH: To be punished where you sinned: in this world. (*To* ALVA.) But maybe she'll be an angel in the next! Howling after the Creator with all this sin in her face! (*He coughs from a hollow chest, raises himself up painfully, coughs again and spits on the floor.*)

LULU: (*Pouring the contents of the basin out the window into a water pipe on the roof.*) To let my face be spat on! To let guys kick me in the belly with their knees!

ALVA: If only there were something to smoke around here! I dream of a cigarette outdoing anything ever smoked, the Ideal Cigarette!

LULU: People you can't see, their hat in their face, their collar over their ears, their hands in their overcoat pockets... Why'm I to go down there? I never cost you a centime. (*Pointing at* ALVA.) There lies a writer, shouldn't *he* do something about it, turn his talents to account?

ALVA: Virago! Who dragged me down in the mud, took my ideals away, strangled the last spark of humanity in me?

LULU: Horse shit.

ALVA: Who made me my father's murderer?

LULU: You, did *you* shoot him?

ALVA: She wants all the credit for herself.

LULU: Good for NOTHING. The sight of you makes me want to cut my hands off. *He* lost nothing, he had nothing left to lose. But in comparison with you, God in Heaven!

ALVA: I'm what you've made me.

LULU: Did *I* run after *you*?

ALVA: My little Marie, if I think back, so good, so cheerful, that child, a dove too good for any man, full of joy yet totally undemanding...I showed her the door for this she-wolf's sake! —Success, one success after another opening up before me, no man was ever offered a more brilliant future. I was on the way to becoming one of the outstanding men of our day—all squandered, frittered away, gone with the wind!

SCHIGOLCH: He's getting cramps.

ALVA: Waiting for the end. —I've left nothing human untried. —Why *not* starve to death, why not?

LULU: He should seek out some Sister of Mercy.

ALVA: And offer her what you have left of me, my used-up juices, my frightful lechery—

LULU: Milksop.

ALVA: She-wolf! Hyena!

SCHIGOLCH: (*To* LULU.) Don't stand on ceremony, you have everything you need.

LULU: If I start this at all it'll be on my own account.

SCHIGOLCH: Bring us a lord. We'll respect his rank, and sing: God save the Queen!

LULU: And I'll come up in the world again. I can still do *anything*—if I'm alone.

SCHIGOLCH: A bit of Christmas Pudding would satisfy *my* needs.

LULU: I'm not earning English Guineas for the benefit of you two.

ALVA: Haven't *I* prostituted myself all a man could?

SCHIGOLCH: Ja, ja.

ALVA: Those charts I drafted, brooding all night, calculations based on the laws of the universe. —Money got away from me like I'd thrown it out the window.

SCHIGOLCH: Ja, ja.

LULU: (*To* SCHIGOLCH.) He got himself good and cheated by men and women alike.

SCHIGOLCH: I don't understand women.

ALVA: I never did understand them.

LULU: I understand them.

SCHIGOLCH: It's like he was made of Dresden china: No hair on his chest...

ALVA: I offered myself to them...for sale...

SCHIGOLCH: Little, mother-of-pearl ears. —I know what *I* want: Pudding, a bit of Christmas pudding.

ALVA: Each one threw me into the arms of another, not to mention the *feet* of these English ladies. —Englishmen have their womenfolk: they make it up to *them* for their orgies with the likes of us.

LULU: He's such a weak sister, he couldn't tame a dog.

ALVA: Tried everything. —In Paris, they get to you. —I could read their wishes in their eyes. —There was this woman— she wanted money for it afterwards—she breaks my umbrella in two—I call a policeman—she grabs a handful of fresh apples off the street and throws them in my face. — They call'em Daughters of Joy hereabouts. —I've spared myself no disappointment. —Better to die of hunger, better to freeze, than to ask those priestesses to be human!

SCHIGOLCH: When you're young, you don't make heavy weather of dying.

ALVA: Since we came up in this loft, I've never sniffed at a woman. Who would've known it would come to this? But now, when I crack my jokes, women just laugh. When I try the natural approach, they slap my face. When I come on bestial, they discover chastity, move to the next table, and let me sing to empty chairs. —The less a guy gets to eat, the more the fire eats him. Lust. —Katya! You are a fright: but if one must choose between you and madness... (*He pulls himself up and staggers in torn pants over to* LULU.)

LULU: (*Taking hold of his outstretched hands, wrestles him to the ground, and throws him on his back.*) First let'em take you to the hospital.

ALVA: Who made me sick?

LULU: Am *I* sick?

ALVA: (*On all fours, head out and up.*) No, no, you're not sick, you're well and you're gonna make many a guy happy!

SCHIGOLCH: Don't keep your dependents crying out for bread all this time...

ALVA: You are not sick.

LULU: I've kept myself clean all my life—only to drown in filth. (*She sits down at the foot of* SCHIGOLCH's *mattress and props her elbows on her knees.*)

SCHIGOLCH: She's waiting till our tongues hang out.

LULU: Warm me!

SCHIGOLCH: Such is the reward for all one's efforts, the sleepless nights, the...*

LULU: I'll bring the blanket.

* In the original, an echo of a Goethe poem ("Wer nie sein Brot...")

ALVA: So what are you afraid of, healthy like you are?

SCHIGOLCH: She's still waiting for that virgin's myrtle wreath without which no preacher will marry her to anyone.

ALVA: (*Struggling up from the floor.*) I'm gonna do you in. You've brought me to this. You bloodhound bitch. I'm gonna do you in and get me a bellyful of your blood! (*But he drags himself back on to his bed.*)

LULU: (*To* SCHIGOLCH.) Unbutton your coat, just let me get my feet in there...

SCHIGOLCH: If only you still had Indian-silk panties—with garters—

LULU: Please.

SCHIGOLCH: They're worth quite a bit—Bit of pudding for me, though.

LULU: I'm still what I am.

SCHIGOLCH: Ja, Ja.

LULU: Unbutton. Please. I'm dying of cold.

SCHIGOLCH: For that matter, *I* could go at any moment. My fingertips have been dead ever since Paris, and they get bluer every day. —What I'd like, as I say, is one last Christmas pudding. —Toward midnight I'll be looking in at the club downstairs, call it travel fever. Maybe they'll be gambling, I don't like that. But hovering behind the bar: a lovely blond Miss!

LULU: (*Pointing at the three of them.*) For Christ's sake! (*She goes to the flower table and puts the whisky bottle to her lips.*)

SCHIGOLCH: This way they'll smell you at ten paces. Before you open your mouth.

LULU: (*Putting the bottle down, with a poisonous look at* SCHIGOLCH.) I'm not drinking it all. (*She exits, left.*)

ALVA: (*Wrapping himself in his rug.*) She should've been Empress of Russia, she'd've come into her own, a second Catherine the Great.

(*Pause.*)

LULU: (*Comes back in with a pair of worn-out booties from the left and sits on the chair near the door, stammering.*) I hope I won't fall down those stairs but I do feel...yeah, I gotta laugh—je jouerai, je jouerai—(*Stamping on the floor in her boots.*) Hoo! Is that cold! —I gotta—(*She goes to the flower table and picks up the bottle.*)

SCHIGOLCH: No dog in London would even piss on her.

LULU: (*Putting the bottle down.*) Ça m'excite! —(*She takes another swallow and totters off at Center.*)

SCENE TWO. Schigolch. Alva.

ALVA: Terrible pity about her, as I think back.

(*Pause.*)

SCHIGOLCH: When we hear them coming we must creep into this little hole of mine for a while.

ALVA: You could say we grew up together.

(*Long pause.*)

SCHIGOLCH: She's lasting as long as I do!

ALVA: When I met her—the first time—She was getting dressed. We were brother and sister from the beginning—she was on a rocking chair in her chemise—Turkish slippers on her feet having her hair done. Dr. Goll had been called out to perform an operation. This was in Mama's lifetime. My first poem had appeared in "Viennese Fashion:" TO A CRUEL BELOVED.

> Over the hills, O huntress fleet,
> Run your beagle pack!
> When they come back
> Covered, I'll bet
> With dust and sweat
> Get out your whip
> And let'er rip!
> They'll whimper and lick your feet.*

---

* "To a Cruel Beloved" is of course one of Wedekind's own poems, the first stanza of which is translated here.

SCHIGOLCH: Ja. ja.

(*Pause.*)

ALVA: Then it was the Museum Ball. She was in pink tulle, white bodice underneath. Papa arranged it all. She entered with Dr. Goll, they weren't married yet. Mama was there too, decided at the last moment, she'd had a headache all day. Papa didn't want to go to *her*, so I had to go on the floor and dance. Papa never looked away all evening. Later she shot him. Frightful.

SCHIGOLCH: Today I wonder if anyone will still bite?

ALVA: I was there. I wouldn't advise'em to.

SCHIGOLCH: What an idiot!

(*Pause.*)

ALVA: Three years younger than me. Even so she behaved like a mother to me. Of course she *was* my stepmother. My little sister. Papa had sent her to the Pension —my wife, ooh!

SCHIGOLCH: I hope she won't run again.

ALVA: Later, when she was married to Schwarz the painter for a couple of months, she saw something in me, something better, higher. She talked to me about my spiritual problems. It didn't last. —I made love to her the first time in her bridal dress, the day of her wedding with Papa, she'd got the two of us mixed up.

SCHIGOLCH: Here they come. (*Heavy steps are heard on the stairs.*)

ALVA: (*Getting up.*) She mustn't do this.

SCHIGOLCH: (*Getting out of bed with difficulty.*) Forward!

ALVA: (*Standing on his chaise longue, throwing the rug about his hips.*) I'll throw the dog to the ground.

SCHIGOLCH: (*Dragging himself right across the room and taking* ALVA *by the arm.*) Forward march! He can't pour his heart out to her with us lounging around.

ALVA: Leave me alone, I'd rather kill myself than...

SCHIGOLCH: Baa lamb! Fop! Bum! Will you feed your family? (*Pushes him downstage right.*)

ALVA: (*Threatening.*) But if he threatens her with...filth?

SCHIGOLCH: What then?

ALVA: Heaven have mercy upon him.

SCHIGOLCH: Forward march! (*He pushes him into the den.*)

ALVA: We must leave the door open.

SCHIGOLCH: (*Going into the den with* ALVA.) *You* don't hear anything anyway.

ALVA: I'll hear.

SCHIGOLCH: Now keep your trap shut.

ALVA: Heaven have mercy upon him.

SCENE THREE. Lulu. Mr. Hopkins. The foregoing.

LULU: (*Opens the door and lets* MR. HOPKINS *in.*) Here is my little room. (MR. HOPKINS *is a giant: rosy clean shaven face, sky blue eyes, a friendly smile playing on his lips. He wears a top hat and a long formal coat and is carrying a dripping umbrella. He places his index finger on his lips and gazes intently at* LULU.)

LULU: It's none too comfortable here. (MR. HOPKINS *places her hand in front of her mouth.*)

LULU: What do you mean? (MR. HOPKINS *places her hand in front of her mouth and his index finger to his lips.*)

LULU: I don't understand. (MR. HOPKINS *holds her lips together.*)

LULU: (*Pulling free.*) We are alone, there's no one...(MR. HOPKINS *holds her lips together. Then he walks to the back neatly folds his coat and hangs it on a chair near the door, opens his umbrella lays it on the floor to dry.*)

SCHIGOLCH: (*To* ALVA, *behind the half-open door downstage right.*) This guy is weird.

ALVA: He better watch out!

SCHIGOLCH: She could hardly have found us a lousier type. (MR. HOPKINS *walks forward with a grin, takes* LULU'*s head in both hands and kisses her forehead.*)

LULU: (*Taking a step back.*) I hope you're coming up with some money.

(MR. HOPKINS *holds her lips together and presses half a sovereign into her hand.* LULU *checks it out, tossing it from one hand to the other.* MR. HOPKINS *gives an uncertain, questioning look.* LULU *sticks the half sovereign in her pocket.*)

LULU: All right. (MR. HOPKINS *holds her lips together, gives her two half crowns, and throws an imperious look her way.*)

LULU: You are generous.

(MR. HOPKINS *jumps about the room like a madman, gesticulating with his arms in the air, and staring despairingly at the sky.* LULU *goes up to him, encircles his waist with her arm, places her index finger on her lips, and shakes her head to say no.* MR. HOPKINS *takes her head in both his hands and kisses her on the mouth.* LULU *encircles his neck, presses herself against him, and gives him a long kiss on the mouth. Laughing soundlessly,* MR. HOPKINS *breaks free from her and gives a questioning look at the chaise longue on the left and the mattress on the right.* LULU *takes the lamp from the flower table, throws* MR. HOPKINS *a look that is full of promise, and opens the door downstage left.* MR. HOPKINS *nods and goes in with a smile, taking off his hat in the doorway.* LULU *follows. The stage is dark except for a beam of light from a crack in the doorway on the left.*)

ALVA: (*In the half-open door on the right, on all fours.*) They're in there.

SCHIGOLCH: Wait.

ALVA: Can't hear anything here.

SCHIGOLCH: Idiot.

ALVA: I'm going to the door. (LULU *enters on the left, lamp in hand. She smiles and shakes her head. She takes the rug from the chaise longue and is going to pick up the wash basin from the floor but when she notices* SCHIGOLCH *and* ALVA *she is startled and signals to them to stay inside.*)

SCHIGOLCH: (*Sharply.*) Tell me he didn't give you fake money. (*Conveying timid pleas,* LULU *puts her index finger to her lips*

*and knits her brow, takes the wash basin from the spot where it
catches the raindrops, and exits left, closing the door behind
her.*)

ALVA: Now—

SCHIGOLCH: Idiot. (*He presses past* ALVA, *gropes his way across the
stage, takes the coat off the chair and goes through its pockets.*
ALVA *has slipped across to* LULU'*s door.*)

SCHIGOLCH: Gloves. —Nothing. (*He turns the coat inside out and
goes through the inside pockets, takes out a book, holds it in the
beam of light, and painfully deciphers the title page.*) "Lessons
for Christian Workers, preface by the Reverend W. Hay,—
Very helpful. —Price three shillings and sixpence." (*Putting
the book back in the coat.*) This guy is nuts. (*He puts the coat
back on the chair.*)

ALVA: Now—

SCHIGOLCH: (*Groping his way back, downstage right.*) There's
NOTHING here in London, this nation's greatness is a
thing of the past. (*In the doorway downstage right, whispering
across to* ALVA.) How's it goin'?

ALVA: (*After a pause.*) He's getting dressed.

SCHIGOLCH: The world is never as bad as one imagines.

ALVA: My wife, my wife. (*He creeps back to the right and pulls*
SCHIGOLCH *with him into the den.*)

SCHIGOLCH: The guy hasn't got so much as a silk hanky.

ALVA: Quiet now.

SCHIGOLCH: And we Germans are crawling on our bellies before
such people!

ALVA: His weapon is a repeater.

SCHIGOLCH: All that for tuppence?

ALVA: He's very grand, I envy him that.

SCHIGOLCH: Oh, me too, me too. (MR. HOPKINS *comes back on
from the left,* LULU *following him with the lamp. They look at
each other.*)

LULU: Are you gonna come here again? (MR. HOPKINS *holds her lips shut.* LULU, *in a kind of dream, looks with a kind of desperation at the sky and nervously shakes her head.* MR. HOPKINS *has thrown his cloak over his shoulders and approaches her now with a grin. She throws herself on his neck. He quietly tears himself free, kisses her hand, and turns toward the door. She makes as if to accompany him but he signals to her to stay behind. He exits stage center.)*

SCENE FOUR. Lulu. Schigolch. Alva.

LULU: (*Coming forward.*) He wore me out, that man, just—

SCHIGOLCH: How much did you get?

LULU: Wore me out. (*Puts the lamp on the flower stand.*) I must go downstairs.

ALVA: (*Blocking her path.*) Not again. No.

LULU: Shut your—O God, O God.

SCHIGOLCH: She's reached that stage, the Holy Spirit has descended! I prophesied this.

LULU: (*Throwing her arms back.*) I can't stand it.

SCHIGOLCH: Always a good sign. We're on our way. How much did you get?

LULU: (*Pushing* ALVA *aside.*) I have to, I can't help it. (*She stands rooted to the spot.*)

ALVA: What's that?

LULU: He's coming back.

SCHIGOLCH: (*Taking* ALVA *by the sleeve.*) Come.

LULU: It's someone else.

ALVA: Who? Who *can* it be?

SCHIGOLCH: Come.

LULU: God knows.

ALVA: I think it's—(*A knock. The three look at each other. The door is opened from the outside.*)

SCENE FIVE. Geschwitz. The foregoing.

LULU: You?!

GESCHWITZ: (*Her face sunken and sallow, in shabby clothes, a rolled canvas in her hand.*) If it's not convenient—

LULU: So late.

GESCHWITZ: I've not spoken with a soul in nine days.

LULU: But did you—?

GESCHWITZ: (*Her eyes on the floor.*) No...nothing—

LULU: (*Her chin out, goes downstage left.*) I can't stand it.

SCHIGOLCH: Your Grace merely wishes to ask how we're doing.

GESCHWITZ: I did write to my brother. He sent nothing.

LULU: Confined to barracks...

GESCHWITZ: Today I hadn't enough money to buy something to eat.

SCHIGOLCH: So you'd like to stretch your legs under *our* table. (*He approaches* GESCHWITZ *and touches the canvas roll.*)

GESCHWITZ: Lulu—

LULU: I must go downstairs now.

GESCHWITZ: Lulu—

LULU: I'll be right back.

SCHIGOLCH: What *is* that ?

GESCHWITZ: (*To* LULU.) I have it.

LULU: I'm going crazy.

GESCHWITZ: The picture.

ALVA: What? You have her portrait?

LULU: (*At the door.*) I'll jump in the Thames if no one takes pity on me.

ALVA: (*Has taken the picture from* GESCHWITZ *and unrolled it.*) There! We have it back!

LULU: (*Coming forward.*) What is that?

GESCHWITZ: Your picture.

ALVA: I think it's faded a bit.

LULU: (*Crying out.*) Oh! Oh, God in heaven!

SCHIGOLCH: We must pin it up.

ALVA: (*To* GESCHWITZ.) How did you come by it?

SCHIGOLCH: It'll make a good impression on our customers.

GESCHWITZ: I cut it out of the frame. —The day after I sneaked upstairs.

ALVA: There's a nail that'll do. (*Attaches the picture to a nail in the wall.*)

GESCHWITZ: It's cracked in places, I had no better way of carrying it.

SCHIGOLCH: It needs another nail underneath.

ALVA: Let me. (*Extracts a nail from the wall, takes off one boot, then hammers in the nail at the bottom of the picture with this boot.*)

SCHIGOLCH: It'll be all right, it was rolled up too long.

GESCHWITZ: A dealer in Drury Lane offered me half a crown for it on sight, I didn't let him have it.

ALVA: (*Putting the boot back on.*) Now it must hang for a while.

SCHIGOLCH: The whole place thereby gets a new look—more fashionable.

ALVA: (*Stepping back, to* LULU.) The lamp, my child. (LULU *comes with lamp.*)

SCHIGOLCH: When they see this, they'll appreciate being here!

ALVA: She had everything that could make a man happy. (LULU *laughs.*)

SCHIGOLCH: What's not there any more—you can think it. (LULU *laughs.*)

ALVA: She's lost weight.

SCHIGOLCH: Who hasn't? That's the way it goes.

ALVA: The eyes are still the same.

SCHIGOLCH: She ate nothing but goose liver at the time. —Just look at those arms.

ALVA: The magnificent bust. —It was just before her very best time.

SCHIGOLCH: At least she can say: that was me. (LULU *laughs.*)

ALVA: So exact a likeness, fascinating. Attitude, lines, the skin fresh as morning dew...

GESCHWITZ: Must have been an extremely gifted painter. (LULU *laughs.*)

ALVA: (*To* GESCHWITZ.) Didn't *you* know him?

GESCHWITZ: No. It was before my time.

SCHIGOLCH: And what legs! Legs don't come like that any more. (LULU *laughs.*)

ALVA: And the subtle smile on the face! Enough to heave the world off its hinges.

SCHIGOLCH: Her guys today will never be able to imagine...

ALVA: The whiteness touched with pink! The luster—you see it in flashes—as if air had crystallized in drops!

SCHIGOLCH: Her whole body—a beam of light. (LULU *laughs.*)

ALVA: Joy in every joint, that's what this girl feels. Love-longing underneath—and on top, daybreak. You don't see lips, you see kisses.

SCHIGOLCH: It sure is a heavenly boon, this picture. Woman herself is here today and gone tomorrow.

ALVA: The old enthusiasm for her returns! (LULU *laughs.*) The picture clarifies my whole fate.

SCHIGOLCH: I've known that mouth since her milk teeth came out!

ALVA: When you live together year in, year out, you don't notice the decline.

SCHIGOLCH: Back then I let myself be looked at in the light of day. Back then I had some gal pining for me on every other block.

ALVA: I'm getting my self-respect back.

SCHIGOLCH: But now that's all gone with the garbage truck. — Those were the days when—

ALVA: The deception with which nature gets the better of us! Woman blooms for precisely those few seconds in which she'll deceive someone for a lifetime.

SCHIGOLCH: *She* don't need deception any more. She can stand up under a street lamp with a dozen English chatterboxes looking on.

ALVA: To be caught in traps set by Providence itself is no contemptible destiny.

SCHIGOLCH: Late in the evening, when you feel the need, you don't ask questions about physical charms.

ALVA: In what woman did nature ever fight with more powerful means?

SCHIGOLCH: What do you ask of a girl's eyes? Only that they not be the eyes of a thief. So you're not looking at her body, you're wondering about her soul.

ALVA: People who've been spared my misery have missed out on my...beatitude.

SCHIGOLCH: We're long in the tooth, you and I. People who spend money usually have reason to. But folks who are over the hill are too smart to come up with cash. —She's not as dumb as she wants us to think, am I right, my girl?

LULU: (*Setting the lamp down on the flower table.*) I'll be right back.

ALVA: You're not going!

GESCHWITZ: Where'd you propose to go?

LULU: Out—out...

ALVA: To prostitute herself.

GESCHWITZ: (*Crying out.*) Lulu!

LULU: (*Tears in her eyes.*) I have misery enough, don't!

GESCHWITZ: Lulu, Lulu, I'm coming with you—wherever!

SCHIGOLCH: That's all we need.

GESCHWITZ: (*Falling at* LULU's *feet.*) Come with me. I'll go to work for you.

LULU: Get away from me, monster.

GESCHWITZ: I'll take your place.

SCHIGOLCH: (*Stepping on* GESCHWITZ'*fingers.*) If you want to put your carcass on view for money, God be with you, quench a hundred years of thirst but—

GESCHWITZ: Lulu, Lulu!

SCHIGOLCH: Don't scare Albion's sons away from *us*! —No fishing in our pond! Find some other block! (LULU *has hurried downstairs.*)

GESCHWITZ: (*Picking herself up.*) I'll never leave her side. I have weapons...(*She runs after her.*)

SCHIGOLCH: Cripes, cripes, cripes.

SCENE SIX. Alva. Schigolch.

ALVA: (*Tossing on the chaise longue.*) I have little to look forward to.

SCHIGOLCH: Why didn't you take her by the throat?

ALVA: I'm burned out. My skin, my soul: dead coals.

SCHIGOLCH: She attacks everything that lives. Like rat poison. Her with her philosophical nose...

ALVA: She threw me on my back and stuck thorns in me.

SCHIGOLCH: But we shouldn't be ungrateful.

ALVA: She ate away at me like an ulcer.

SCHIGOLCH: (*Stretching out on his mattress.*) But hers was the gentle hand of Providence, It was Geschwitz who brought Rodrigo Quast to the Rue de la Gare.

ALVA: How gracefully he welcomed the *coup the grâce*?

SCHIGOLCH: Rodrigo Quast: the bathroom bridegroom!

ALVA: Hovering over me—like golden apples over the head of Tantalus!

SCHIGOLCH: The countess had let him rob her of her fossilized virginity!

ALVA: And what has Katya made of me? Poisons and parasites celebrate their Babylonian orgies in me!

(*Pause.*)

SCHIGOLCH: You can turn up the lamp a bit.

ALVA: There's something frightening in one's own dissolution.

SCHIGOLCH: When *I* was twenty-three I knew how to take care of myself...

ALVA: I wonder if a simple child of nature could suffer the way I do.

SCHIGOLCH: Even if I'd nothing but a necktie to cover my nakedness.

ALVA: Not everyone has tasted such a gilded youth as mine.

SCHIGOLCH: The lamp's going out, fast.

ALVA: So much the better.

SCHIGOLCH: At one time I had my three houses in the new section of Heinrich Strasse. —But you get used to doing without,

ALVA: To think what I've made of my life!

SCHIGOLCH: Does it have to be so dark in here till she comes?

ALVA: The years pass 'till you hardly recall any particular moment.

SCHIGOLCH: Just look what this filthy weather has made of my cap and bells, so to speak.

ALVA: You can't hear the rain any more.

SCHIGOLCH: I hope those two haven't stayed together.

ALVA: Looks like it'll be nice weather in the morning.

SCHIGOLCH: A fellow doesn't go with two at a time.

ALVA: They *can't* have stayed together.

SCHIGOLCH: Thank God she has enough sense to chase her away with her fists.

ALVA: I recall two guys. One won the admiration of the whole nation...

SCHIGOLCH: I think...I hear something...

ALVA: The other is now in London's lower depths unable to die.

SCHIGOLCH: Doncha hear anything?

ALVA: From where? —And they'd spend such happy hours together—hours of creative pleasure, hours of dazzling hopes for the future.

SCHIGOLCH: They're coming, they're coming.

ALVA: Who?

SCHIGOLCH: (*Getting up.*) Madame la Comtesse!

ALVA: I'm staying.

SCHIGOLCH: Lunkhead.

ALVA: Staying. I'll crawl under the rug, at least I'll be on hand.

SCHIGOLCH: Mother's boy! (*He crawls into his den downstage right and closes the door behind him.*)

SCENE SEVEN. Kungu Poti,* Crown Prince of Ouah-Oubay. Lulu. Alva.

ALVA *creeps under his rug.*

LULU: (*Opening the door.*) Come in, come in.

KUNGU POTI: (*In light-colored top hat, light overcoat, and light pants, stumbling up the stairs.*) It's very dark here.

LULU: Come in, darling, there's more light here.

KUNGU POTI: Is this your sitting room?

LULU: (*Closing the door.*) You're so serious!

KUNGU POTI: I'm cold,

LULU: Want a drink?

KUNGU POTI: Got any brandy?

LULU: Whiskey. (*Taking the bottle.*) I don't know where there's a glass.

KUNGU POTI: No matter. (*He takes the bottle.*)

LULU: (*To herself.*) He looks like a burnt pancake.

KUNGU POTI: What?

LULU: You look like such a nice man.

KUNGU POTI: Think so?

LULU: Yes. (*To herself.*) On the street, he didn't look so dark.

KUNGU POTI: My father is Sultan of Ouah-Oubay.

* A "crown prince" who is later called a "nigger" by Lulu and who also describes himself as a Sultan's son ("Kungu" and "Ouah" are African place names). He may, of course, be an impostor, lying about both his name and background. The other three johns in this Act never provide their names. Since, therefore a theatre audience never finds out "who they are," it would be best in any theatre program to list johns simply as johns (or customers) 1, 2, 3, and 4.

LULU: Is he? How many wives does he have?

KUNGU POTI: Only four. Here in London, I have six. Three English, three French. But I don't like to deal with them.

LULU: You're not on good terms with them?

KUNGU POTI: High style I don't like.

LULU: You'd rather come here—with me?

KUNGU POTI: That's right.

LULU: (*To herself.*) And he smells of menagerie.

KUNGU POTI: What?

LULU: Will you be staying long in London?

KUNGU POTI: I must return to Ouah-Oubay when my father dies.

LULU: Where you will then do what?

KUNGU POTI: Be king of my country—which is twice as big as England. But I'd rather stay here.

LULU: I believe you. How much will you be giving me?

KUNGU POTI: What's your name?

LULU: Daisy.

KUNGU POTI: (*Sings and does a few kicks.*) "Daisy. Daisy / Give me your answer, do!"

LULU: Wait: How much will you be paying?

KUNGU POTI: One sovereign—Daisy. (*Continuing his act.*) "I'm half crazy / All for the love of you!" (*He tries to kiss her.*)

LULU: (*Fending him off.*) Let me see your money.

KUNGU POTI: One pound. I pay with a gold sovereign.

LULU: You can pay later, but show it to me.

KUNGU POTI: Never I pay beforehand!

LULU: All right, but show it to me.

KUNGU POTI: No! Now, Daisy—

LULU: Then please go.

KUNGU POTI: (*Taking hold of her.*) Come—

LULU: Let go of me!

KUNGU POTI: (*Holding her hair.*) Come! Where's the bed?

LULU: (*Crying out.*) No! Don't do that! (KUNGU POTI *throws her to the floor.* ALVA *has emerged from under the rug and is proceeding slowly forward to take* KUNGU POTI *by the throat.*)

LULU: (*Crying out loudly.*) Holy God!

(KUNGU POTI *reaches into his pocket, then hits* ALVA *on the head.*)

ALVA: (*Collapsing.*) Mama!

KUNGU POTI: What a dump! A slaughter house. I'm off! (*He leaves by the center door.*)

LULU: (*Getting up.*) So there goes...Alva. —I must be on my way. Why did I have to bring in a black man with all those whites to choose from? Y'only have to ask, "Do you have the time?" Start a conversation. "Out so late? And so *sad,* why so sad?" Yeah, Yeah. (*She exits center stage.*)

SCENE EIGHT. Schigolch. Alva.

SCHIGOLCH: (*Comes fumblingly in on the right, bends over* ALVA.) That's what you get, meddling in other folk's love affairs. (*Feeling his head.*) Blood. (*Goes to the table and comes back with the lamp.*) Can't see a thing. —Alva! —His eardrums must be made of parchment. (*He puts down the lamp and presses his ear against* ALVA'*s back.*) It's buzzing. (*Turns him over and feels his temples.*) No fever, he's cool. (*Shouts into his ear.*) Alva, Alva! (*Lifting the left eyelid with his thumbs.*) I know, I know. (*Taking* ALVA'*s head in both hands and feeling it.*) The cannibal. Deep, deep. (*He lets the head drop, it bangs on the floor.*) Oops! —We must put him to bed. (*He tries to lift him, with one arm under his shoulders, the other under his knees, but lets him drop. Picking himself up.*) The kid doesn't weigh much—if there were only someone to help me—(*Bending over* ALVA.) So say something, you were never the silent type. —Don't be so sleepy, the whole world is before you! (*Shaking him.*) Come, come! Don't take it to heart so, he didn't mean any harm. A hundred times and more you'll still—Don't be so dumb, it isn't worth the trouble, you're still too young for this life! Come on, be reasonable! (*Getting up.*) Who won't be advised cannot be helped. —He wants to mull it over for a while. —He's smiling like some guy had stuck a lump of sugar in his mouth! (*Picks him up again in the same manner and this time manages to drag him a few steps to the left. Setting him down.*) What price those dazzling hopes for the future now?...Don't you hear ANYTHING I say? (*Gives him a box on the ear.*) Just driving out your whims and caprices! (*Picking him up again.*) He wants to be left in peace. (*Drags him to* LULU's *room, left. Pause. Returns, picks the lamp up off the floor, and sets it down on the flower stand.*) This, too, hasn't long to go. (*He turns up the lamp to look at* LULU's *portrait.*)—It still isn't hanging quite like it should. —It has something—the white legs—one arm in the air—like death. It pops up in a man's dreams. —And bit by bit our time will come. —God knows when she will return from her little expedition,—When a guy's lived as long as yours truly, seen things flare up and then fall flat, he don't jump in the Thames...(*Goes into his den and comes back wearing a battered bristly old top hat.*) No, he buys himself some Scotch Whiskey and eats some Christmas pudding...(*Startled.*) Good God, someone's coming...

SCENE NINE. Schigolch. Geschwitz.

GESCHWITZ *opens the door without a sound.*

SCHIGOLCH: You.
GESCHWITZ: Me.
SCHIGOLCH: I thought maybe it was him...
GESCHWITZ: He's coming.
SCHIGOLCH: (*Moving to the door.*) I won't disturb him.

GESCHWITZ: I won't keep you.

SCHIGOLCH: I'll take my leave. Say hello to...

GESCHWITZ: How dark it's getting!

SCHIGOLCH: It'll get darker.

GESCHWITZ: I'm...deformed.

SCHIGOLCH: All things end sometime.

GESCHWITZ: I can't take it.

SCHIGOLCH: I still can, thank God.

GESCHWITZ: Can't leave. Can't stay.

SCHIGOLCH: You think you can be father of a family just 'cause you're flat chested.

GESCHWITZ: I've learned to wait.

SCHIGOLCH: Go ahead and wait, it's certainly more reasonable than trying to compete with her. —Maybe you'll even grow...(*He indicates a bosom she does not at present have.*)

GESCHWITZ: She sent me on ahead.

SCHIGOLCH: Then I'll be meeting her on my way out. (*Exit at center.*)

SCENE TEN. Geschwitz.

GESCHWITZ: (*Alone.*) Deformed. She called me deformed. (*Sitting on a wicker chair near the door.*) Maybe she *has* something. —I've waited three years. —She used me as a deadly weapon and deceived me. It was outright deception. —I've waited all of three years for that one minute. —Now if she were to see me in the throes of death—my life's all I have now, she's taken everything else—the papers—shares—bonds—rents—my part of the family estate at Geschwitz—my honor—my happiness—But I'll wait: what do I have if I'm dead? —She doesn't weep. —I've lost all belief in God. —Deformed—by whom? —By myself—all these years. Well then, if I'm deformed, perverted, when *he* comes in, I'll shoot him down. Every one of 'em is hale and hearty, every little twerp off the street, every one of 'em can arouse her. Just me—I can't! —In the whole population of the world! —Why? Why must *I* be under this curse? (*Long pause.*)

SCENE ELEVEN. Lulu. Dr. Hilti.* Geschwitz.

GESCHWITZ *sits motionless by the door unnoticed by the other two.* LULU *opens the door and lets in* DR. HILTI.

LULU: So late, Sir, where've you been?

DR. HILTI: At the theater.

LULU: Which one?

DR. HILTI: The Alhambra.

LULU: Ah yes! The dancers!

DR. HILTI: I never saw such lovely girls!

LULU: Prettily dressed—

DR. HILTI: Two thousand ladies lifting up their right leg, all at the same time.

LULU: You saw that?

DR. HILTI: Indeed. Then two thousand ladies lifted up their left leg, all at the same time. New to me, such girls.

LULU: Are you English?

DR. HILTI: Swiss. I've only been here two weeks. How about you?

LULU: Well, sir, I am...French.

DR. HILTI: Ah, vous êtes française?

LULU: Oui, Monsieur, je suis Parisienne.

DR. HILTI: Vraiment?

LULU: Une vraie Parisienne. My mother's the cashier at Café Calypso, she used to sell fish on Boulevard Rochechouart. My father belongs to the highest nobility, I only saw him once, I was fifteen, he lived in the Faubourg St. Honoré, a

---

* In the original, Dr. Hilti speaks a dialect, Swiss German, a form of speech Wedekind found amusing. Also, at the beginning of the scene, Lulu has some difficulty finding out what language to speak to him in. Consequently not everything from the original would make sense in a rendering which, except for a few words of French, is all in English.

hundred horses in his stables.

DR. HILTI: I've just come from Paris. I was there eight days.

LULU: On s'y amuse mieux qu'ici, vous ne trouvez pas?

DR. HILTI: Mais oui, in Paris I was in the Louvre daily.

LULU: Doing what?!

DR. HILTI: Admiring the pictures.

LULU: So c'mon over to the chaise longue, you're gonna stay all night, you have lovely eyes. (*She kisses him.*)

DR. HILTI: I've only five shillings on me.

LULU: Let's take a look.

DR. HILTI: (*Emptying his wallet.*) I never carry more.

LULU: (*Taking the money and pocketing it.*) C'est assez, parce-que c'est toi, parce-que tu as des yeux si doux, embrasse-moi!

DR. HILTI: O mon Dieu, my heavens, the devil, hell...

LULU: (*Kissing his mouth.*) Just close this thing up, all right?

DR. HILTI: But this is the first time I've been with a girl.

LULU: Liar! Don't give me that!

DR. HILTI: Hell, you better believe me. I didn't know what to expect.

LULU: Why did you get married so early?

DR. HILTI: Married? I'm NOT married!

LULU: Come on.

DR. HILTI: Mon Dieu, I tell you true.

LULU: What do you do?

DR. HILTI: I'm a Lecturer.

LULU: Oh, come, you should be ashamed.

DR. HILTI: Of what?

LULU: Telling such tales.

DR. HILTI: Heaven and hell. I teach young people.

LULU: Good God. I'm having no luck this evening.

DR. HILTI: Heavens above, you don't understand. I'm a philosopher. I teach philosophy at the university.

LULU: You have the air of a child but you explain yourself like a pimp. —Is it true you've never slept with a woman?

DR. HILTI: Cross my heart. I'm an aristocrat. Very old Swiss family. As a student, I only got two francs pocket money, how could I afford it?

LULU: I thought you were a philosopher?

DR. HILTI: That's right, that's right, a Darwinian materialist.

LULU: Well, tell me, aren't there any women over there?

DR. HILTI: In Zurich?

LULU: Yes.

DR. HILTI: Certainly: In Zurich there are fifty-five houses of Joy. But only married men go there.

LULU: This virginity of yours, has it never been in the way?

DR. HILTI: Never! I had better use for my money. It's the married men who can't do without such filth, their wives are so ugly.

LULU: What filth do you Swiss indulge in?

DR. HILTI: Oh, just filth. Like what *you* do.

LULU: Moi, je fais l'amour.

DR. HILTI: Mais oui, l'amour, filth, right?

LULU: It seems you have little respect for your father!

DR. HILTI: Daddikins? He had another end in view. I should box your ears: Daddikins did it to beget children!

LULU: You're the proof, aren't you? —Why do you come to me?

DR. HILTI: I need to. Got engaged just this evening to a girl from Basel. One of the Best Families. She's working here in London as a Governess.

LULU: Attractive?

DR. HILTI: Yes, she has two million. I gotta learn how to do it. If I'm gonna marry her. I'm eager to learn!

LULU: (*Throwing her hair back.*) Quelle chance pour moi! (*Gets up and takes the lamp.*) Eh bien, viens, mon philosophe, nous verrons! (*She takes* DR. HILTI *into her room and locks it from inside.*)

(GESCHWITZ, *draws a small black revolver from her pocket and points it at her own head.* DR. HILTI *tears open the door from inside and rushes out.*)

DR. HILTI: Carcass and carrion!

LULU: (*Lamp in hand, holding his arm by a sleeve.*) Stay with me.

DR. HILTI: A dead man. A corpse. In there.

LULU: (*Clinging to him.*) Stay with me, stay!

DR. HILTI: (*Pulling free.*) There's a corpse in there! Starry heavens! Carcass and carrion!

LULU: (*Embracing his feet.*) Stay with me.

DR. HILTI: Where's the exit? (*Looks round for the exit, notices* GESCHWITZ, *tears his hair.*) That's the devil, that's the devil.

LULU: Please, please, stay!

DR. HILTI: Corpses and corruption! Everlasting hailstones! (*Exits, center.*)

LULU: (*Jumping up.*) Stay, stay, stay...(*She rushes after him.*)

SCENE TWELVE. Geschwitz.

GESCHWITZ: (*Letting the revolver drop.*) Hanging is better. — Then I'd hear nothing more. —What lies ahead for me? Pain, Pain. Or I could jump off the bridge. —The water is cold. My bed is cold, too. —Which is colder, the water or my bed? —In Paris the parapets weren't so high. —One doesn't freeze for long. —I'd be dreaming of her till the last instant. —Hanging is better. —*She's* cold, too. — Stabbing—I could take a knife to myself. —I don't have what it takes. —No, no: nothing along those lines. —How often I've dreamt she was kissing me. —One minute more. —No, no, no: something always interferes. —Hanging is better. I won't cut into my arteries: nothing along those lines,—Poison? I've nothing to do it with. —Hanging is better. —I feel so dirty, dirty, dirty. —Hanging! (*She conceals the revolver.*) I can't shoot myself, I can't jump in the Thames, the water is too pure. —Hanging! —God knows...(*She suddenly jumps up and takes from the wall the strap belonging to the rug, stands on the chair and fastens the strap to a hook in the wall over the door. She ties the strap round her neck and kicks the chair away. But the hook comes loose, and she finds herself unharmed on the floor, discovering the hook, now affixed to the strap.*) There's a curse on my life, a curse, a curse. (*She remains leaning for a while against the wall, then in tearful tones.*) Lulu, Lulu, if...my time...had come, *if* my time had come—it's just a test—if I'm not gonna go right away—Lulu—you need only do it once, let me speak to your heart—you need...open your heart to me just once, and all will be well. —I can wait, I'm gonna wait for that. —But promise me this much, Lulu, you won't let me go just yet, I needn't go before...you've made me happy just once. You could do that, I know. If you didn't, and I'm in the next world, I'll go on suffering there, and God wouldn't want that. He *doesn't* want it, He won't let me go because He wants me happy just once, once. Lulu, listen to Him! Lulu, He's telling you something on my behalf, He's standing by me, so listen to Him, Lulu, He'll punish you if you don't! —(*She drags herself over to* LULU*'s picture, sinks to her knees and with folded hands.*) Angel that I adore, my darling, my star! Who has suffered more, given you more? —I hear the happiness in that laugh of yours! —Who has had more patience? —Your skin is soft as snow. —Your heart is cold. Have mercy on me!

SCENE THIRTEEN. Jack.* Lulu. Geschwitz.

Jack is a stocky figure of a man and moves very flexibly. He has a pale face, inflamed eyes, a scrofulous nose, dark, arched eyebrows, a drooping moustache, a thin goatee beard, shaggy sideburns, fiery red hands, the fingernails much bitten. While speaking he moves from one pose to another and looks down at the floor. He wears a dark

---

* Wedekind wrote Jack's lines in English but English that is improbable even when it is correct. Adjustments had therefore to be made in this scene, as they were in other scenes above where Wedekind used English.

overcoat and a small round felt hat. LULU *lets Jack in, her eyes flashing fire at* GESCHWITZ *as she does so.*

LULU: (*To* GESCHWITZ.) So you're still here?

JACK: Who's this?

LULU: It's my sister, sir.

JACK: Your sister?

LULU: She's mad. —And always at my heels.

GESCHWITZ: (*Crawling back like a dog.*) I didn't hear you coming.

JACK: Will she disturb us?

LULU: No. Stay. Please don't go.

JACK: You have a beautiful mouth. When you speak...

LULU: (*Opening the door, to* GESCHWITZ.) Out! Wait on the stairs!

JACK: Don't send her out. (*And she does not.*)

LULU: (*Closing the door.*) Will you stay, sir?

JACK: How much do you want?

LULU: For the whole night?

JACK: You have a strong, pretty chin, and your lips are like bursting cherries.

LULU: But when you're through, you'll tell me you've got to go home.

JACK: You're a liar.

LULU: My God.

JACK: You know your business. And you're not English, are you?

LULU: German.

JACK: And where does that beautiful mouth come from?

LULU: My mother.

JACK: I might've guessed. —How much?

LULU: Whatever you say.

JACK: My name's not Rothschild.

LULU: Will you stay all night, sir?

JACK: No. Haven't got time.

LULU: You must have some other reason.

JACK: Yes, I'm married.

LULU: Tell her you missed the last bus and had to stay over with a friend.

JACK: Time is money. —How much?

LULU: Oh, a pound...

JACK: Good night. (*He moves to the door.*)

LULU: (*Holding him back.*) Stay, stay. (JACK *walks past* GESCHWITZ *downstage right, opens the door to the den and pokes around in it.*)

LULU: I live with my sister.

JACK: The gall you have.

LULU: No gall at all. You can pay tomorrow morning.

JACK: When I'm asleep, you'll go through my pockets.

LULU: I don't do that.

JACK: Then why do you want me here all night? (LULU *is silent.*) Very suspicious.

LULU: Give me what you wish.

JACK: Your mouth is your best asset.

LULU: A half sovereign. (JACK *laughs and goes to the door.* LULU *holds him back.*) Don't leave, please!

JACK: How much?

LULU: Nothing.

JACK: Nothing? What would *that* mean? (GESCHWITZ *has moved against* JACK. LULU *throws her to the floor.*)

JACK: Let her be. —She's not your sister, she loves you.

LULU: We are sisters—in law.

JACK: (*Approaches* GESCHWITZ *and strokes her brow.*) We're not enemies, are we? We understand each other, don't we, poor beast? (*He pats her cheek.* GESCHWITZ *crawls backwards throwing poisonous looks at him.*)

LULU: Are you a bugger?

JACK: (*Holding* GESCHWITZ *by the strap still around her neck.*) What was that?

LULU: She's insane, as I told you, but if you prefer to go with *her.*

JACK: (*Holding on to* GESCHWITZ, *to* LULU.) Just tell me how much.

LULU: Eight shillings.

JACK: Too much.

LULU: It it's too much—

JACK: How long have you been on the streets?

LULU: Two years.

JACK: I don't believe you.

LULU: Since my last birthday—

JACK: You are a beginner.

LULU: Starting today.

JACK: So how many have you—?

LULU: First there was a madman who covered my mouth and didn't let me get a word out or even a laugh or a groan. Did that arouse me? I could have bitten his nose off.

JACK: Then?

LULU: Will you stay?

JACK: Then?

LULU: Then came a nigger. We had a fight about money. He wanted to pay later.

JACK: Then?

LULU: I'd like *you* to stay all night.

JACK: I pay in advance.

LULU: Money's not what I want.

JACK: And after the black man?

LULU: No one. Yes: a philosopher. Said he'd never touched a woman. Wanted to practice for his wedding night—on me. Swore like a trooper, said he was Swiss, left before anything happened.

JACK: Why?

LULU: Because of the "beast on the floor."

JACK: (*Holding* GESCHWITZ *still.*) Did she attack him?

LULU: No, he was disappointed, that's all, this wasn't what he was looking for.

JACK: Have you ever had a baby?

LULU: No.

JACK: Thought not.

LULU: Why?

JACK: Your mouth is so...fresh still...

LULU: What's so special about my mouth?

JACK: How much then—for all night?

LULU: Five shillings.

JACK: No thanks. Sleep well. (*He is now in the doorway; she stops him there.*) Anyone else live here?

LULU: Just my sister.

JACK: (*Stamping on the floor.*) And the floor below?

LULU: That room is to let.

JACK: How about three shillings?

LULU: Fine.

JACK: I don't have it.

LULU: Two shillings.

JACK: It was the way you walked. I watched you from behind.

LULU: My skirt is torn behind.

JACK: I saw you had a perfect body.

LULU: You saw this from behind?

JACK: I saw how you placed your feet and said to myself: she must have...an expressive mouth.

LULU: You took such a fancy to my mouth!

JACK: True. You are intelligent, generous, ambitious, and your heart's in the right place.

LULU: You're an original.

JACK: I followed you from behind.

LULU: You're staring at me!

JACK: One shilling is all I have.

LULU: You're aroused now, are you?

JACK: It's three years since I slept with a girl.

LULU: Let me have the shilling.

JACK: What have you been living on?

LULU: I had a job as a parlor maid.

JACK: With those hands? (*He points to her delicate skin.*)

LULU: I had a rich friend. Let's see your shilling.

JACK: You're experienced—in the love business.

LULU: Yes.

JACK: (*Producing his wallet.*) I gotta have sixpence change.

LULU: I don't have any pennies.

JACK: Find it. It's for my bus fare tomorrow.

LULU: You're trembling.

JACK: Pennies. Look in your pocket.

LULU: (*Doing so.*) I don't have it.

JACK: Let *me* look.

LULU: (*Producing a ten shilling note.*) This is all the money I have.

JACK: I want it.

LULU: I can change it in the morning.

JACK: Give it here.

LULU: You are richer than me.

JACK: If I'm gonna stay all night—(LULU *gives him the money and takes the lamp from the flower stand.* JACK *notices* LULU*'s picture.*)—So you're—high society! You knew how to take care of yourself!

LULU: (*Downstage right, opening the door to the den.*) This way.

JACK: We won't need the light.

LULU: In the dark?

JACK: Why not? That lamp's going out anyway. And it stinks.

LULU: True. (*And puts the lamp down on the flower stand.*)

JACK: Ugh, that stink. (*He makes as if to put the lamp out.*)

LULU: Let it burn!

JACK: There's a moon!

LULU: So come on in, why don't you?

JACK: I'm scared.

LULU: (*Falling on his neck and kissing him.*) I love you! I won't harm you. What a baby you are! So bashful. Puzzled now? Why don't you look at me?

JACK: I'm not sure I can make it.

LULU: Oh, you're one of those? (*She inserts her hand under his coat.*) I see, I see. You want it to grow. —Don't make me beg anymore, you have nothing to fear: I was never...ill.

JACK: Aren't you ashamed of yourself? Selling your love?

LULU: What was I to do?

JACK: That's such a low down thing.

LULU: You love me!

JACK: I never saw a more beautiful girl on the street.

LULU: (*Holding him in her embrace.*) Come on in: I'm not as bad as I look.

JACK: All right. (*He follows her into the den.*)

SCENE FOURTEEN. Geschwitz.

GESCHWITZ: (*Alone. Writing with her index finger on the floor.*) You planted this love in my heart, child that I worship, I can't help it...my finger's bleeding, I am, I am too hot—there's something else—I must think it over—Lulu...(*The lamp goes out. On the floorboards under the two skylights appear two harsh squares of light. Everything in the room is now clearly visible. Speaking as if in a dream.*) When it gets dark, when it gets dark, she is my only thought, especially when it gets dark. If only she hadn't ever got married—I must think that over—I feel so dirty, dirty, dirty. —I must think that over: if my father had never married, I'd never have seen her—If my mother...One human being makes another...why am I...deformed...I'm not gonna get married. There's just one person I want to know: Lulu. (*Jumping up.*) Oh! Oh! (*A noise on the right.*)

SCENE FIFTEEN. Geschwitz. Lulu. Jack.

LULU *barefoot, in a slip and underskirt, tears the door open, then holds it shut from the outside, crying:* "Help! Help, Martha!"

GESCHWITZ *runs towards the door, draws her revolver and points it. Making sure* LULU *is behind her, she says:* "Get going." *But* JACK *tears the door down from inside and runs a knife into* GESCHWITZ' *body.* GESCHWITZ *fires a shot into the ceiling and collapses with a loud outcry.* JACK *has gone to the outside door.* LULU, *downstage left, cries* "Oh, oh, oh, God." *There is a pause, and* GESCHWITZ, *her head shrinking into her neck and shoulders, offers the revolver to* LULU, *saying just her name as she does so.* JACK *pulls her over by the strap and takes the revolver.* "Police, police," *cries* LULU, *but* JACK *says:* "Quiet!" *and points the gun at her. With a rattle in her throat* GESCHWITZ *gets out the words:* He's...not firing!" JACK *makes a beeline for* LULU *and tries to grab her.* LULU *runs to the exit, but* JACK *is at the door shouting:* "I 've got you." *Falling back,* LULU *cries,* "He's gonna slice me up!" JACK *cries:* "Shut up!" *and then, throwing himself on the floor, tries to bind her feet together.* LULU *escapes into her room downstage left and presses herself against the door from inside. One hears her calling,* "Help, help, police!" *Knife in hand,* JACK *tries to push the door in.* GESCHWITZ *tries to get up and falls on her side, saying* "My angel, my angel," *while* LULU *calls out:* "Murder, help!" JACK, *working on the door, mutters to himself,* "There isn't a finer mouth on all the seven seas!" *The door gives way, he pushes his way in. For a moment one hears nothing but the groaning of* GESCHWITZ. LULU *gives a loud cry,* "No, no, have pity!" JACK *emerges carrying* LULU *by the arms. He heads obliquely across the stage, while* LULU, *her hand pressed against her forehead, continues to cry out:* "Murder, murder, he's ripping me up!" "The bed is occupied," *says* JACK, *as* LULU *shouts as loudly as she can:* "Police!" JACK *sits her down, takes her head firmly in his hands, forcing his thumb between her teeth, and saying:* "I shall now silence you." *But she manages to get away and* JACK *cries:* "God damn!" *as he throws his weight against the outside door. Sweat is dripping from his hair, and his hands are bloody. He is panting from deep in the chest and staring at the floor with eyes jumping out of his head.* "This is hard work," *he says.* LULU *looks wildly around, trembling in every limb, suddenly grabs the whisky bottle, smashes it on the table, and with the broken remains goes after* JACK. *Raising his right leg,* JACK *knocks* LULU *down with the sole of his right foot. She is now on her back, while he stays put.* LULU *curls up on the floor, her knees against her chest, her hands clasping her abdomen. She groans.* GESCHWITZ *calls out,* "I can't help, Lulu." JACK *pulls himself together, lifts* LULU *off the floor, and carries her toward the right.* LULU *cries,* "Martha, he's cutting me up, he's cutting me up! JACK *deposits her in the den.* GESCHWITZ *shouts:* "Help, help, murder, help!" LULU *can only cry:* "Don't," *and groan.* GESCHWITZ *summons the last strength left in her body to get to the door and continue to shout:* "Lulu! Murder! Police!" *After a pause,* JACK *comes back from the right, un-buttons his overcoat, and places a small packet wrapped in newspaper in his inside pocket. He gropes his way obliquely across the stage and disappears in* LULU'*s room.* LULU *is heard whimpering from the den.* GESCHWITZ *cries:* "Lulu, my love!" JACK *comes back from* LULU'*s room with a full washbasin. He sets it down on the flower-stand and washes his hands.*

JACK: What luck! I could never have thought this up. Such a thing happens once in 200 years.

GESCHWITZ: Lulu, are you alive? My angel!

JACK: When I'm dead, and my collection's auctioned off, the London Hospital Museum will pay three hundred pounds for this night's conquest! (*He taps his pocket.*) Students and professors alike will find it an astonishment! —No towel in this place? They're so damn poor!

GESCHWITZ: Speak...Lulu...

JACK: Well! (*He lifts* GESCHWITZ' *dress and dries his hands on her underskirt.*) This monster is quite safe from me. (*To her.*) It'll all be over soon.

SCENE SIXTEEN. Geschwitz.

GESCHWITZ: (*Left alone now, she tries to get closer to the den downstage right, propping herself on her arms, and leaving a thin trail of blood behind.*) To see you once more, just once...once...I love...love...love...the misery...oh,shit...*

—(*Here her elbows collapse under her. She is trying to get out another word or two as she dies.*)

THE END

* The German has the three letters SCH followed by three dots, for which the exact English equivalent would be SH followed by three dots. Some readers have felt that the word SCHEISS does not fit the style of the character or the scene and therefore that Geschwitz should just be represented as muttering meaninglessness here.

INSPECTOR
AND OTHER PLAYS
by Nicolai Gogol

English versions by Eric Bentley

Eric Bentley brings to the attention of Gogol's still growing American public not only a new version of *Inspector*, but three other dramatic works: *The Marriage, Gamblers* and *A Madman's Diary*, the last-named being Bentley's dramatization of a famous Gogol story.

In a critical Preface, Bentley finds all four works to be a Gogolian treatment of love—or lack of love—and by the same token, thoroughly original works of dramatic art.

At the back of the book comes a bonus in the shape of a piece on *Gamblers* by the eminent Polish critic Jan Kott.

A chronology and guide to further reading are also provided.

ISBN: 0-936839-12-0

LIFE IS A DREAM
and Other SPANISH Classics

Edited by Eric Bentley
Translated by Roy Campbell

"The name of Eric Bentley is enough to guarantee the
significance of any book of or about drama."
—Robert Penn Warren

LIFE IS A DREAM
By Calderon de la Barca

FUENTE OVEJUNA
By Lope de Vega

THE TRICKSTER OF SEVILLE
By Tirso de Molina

THE SIEGE OF NUMANTIA
By Miguel de Cervantes

ISBN: 1-55783-006-1

THE MISANTHROPE
and Other FRENCH Classics

Edited by Eric Bentley

"I would recommend Eric Bentley's collection to all
who really care for theatre."
—Harold Clurman

THE MISANTHROPE By Molière
English version by Richard Wilbur

PHAEDRA By Racine
English version by Robert Lowell

THE CID By Corneille
English Version by James Schevill

FIGARO'S MARRIAGE By Beaumarchais
English version by Jacques Barzun

ISBN: 0-936839-19-8

SERVANT OF TWO MASTERS

and Other ITALIAN Classics

Edited by Eric Bentley

"One can almost venture to talk of a revival of the drama of our time, and it is Eric Bentley who gives us this confidence."

—Sir Herbert Read

THE SERVANT OF TWO MASTERS By Goldoni
   English version by Edward Dent

THE KING STAG By Gozzi
   English version by Carl Wildman

THE MANDRAKE By Machiavelli
   English version by Frederick May and Eric Bentley

RUZZANTE RETURNS FROM THE WARS By Beolco
   English version by Angela Ingold and Theodore Hoffman

ISBN: 0-936839-20-1

❦APPLAUSE❦

BEFORE BRECHT

FOUR GERMAN PLAYS

Edited and Translated
by Eric Bentley

"A breath of fresh air in a mausoleum."
—Herbert Blau

LEONCE AND LENA
by George Büchner

LA RONDE
by Arthur Schnitzler

SPRING'S AWAKENING
by Frank Wedekind

THE UNDERPANTS
by Carl Sternheim

ISBN: 1-55783-010-X

THE BRUTE
& OTHER FARCES
BY ANTON CHEKHOV

edited by Eric Bentley

"INDISPENSABLE!"
—Robert Brustein, Director Loeb Drama Center
Harvard University

All the farces of Russia's greatest dramatist are
rendered here in classic lively translations which
audiences and scholars alike applaud on the stage
and in the classroom. The blustering, stuttering
eloquence of Chekhov's unlikely heroes has endured
to shape the voice of contemporary theatre. This
volume presents seven minor masterpieces:

THE HARMFULNESS OF TOBACCO

SWAN SONG

A MARRIAGE PROPOSAL

THE CELEBRATION

A WEDDING

SUMMER IN THE COUNTRY

THE BRUTE

ISBN: 1-55783-004-5

THE LIFE OF THE DRAMA

by ERIC BENTLEY

"The most adventurous critic in America."

—Kenneth Tynan

"Eric Bentley's radical new look at the grammar of theatre...is a work of exceptional virtue, and readers who find more in it to disagree with than I do will still, I think, want to call it CENTRAL, INDISPENSABLE...If you see any crucial interest in such topics as the death of Cordelia, Godot's non-arrival...THIS IS A BOOK TO BE READ AGAIN AND AGAIN."

—Frank Kermode, *The New York Review of Books*

"*The Life Of The Drama*...is a remarkable exploration of the roots and bases of dramatic art, THE MOST FAR REACHING AND REVELATORY WE HAVE HAD."

—Richard Gilman, *Book Week*

ISBN: 1-55783-110-6

IN SEARCH OF THEATER

by ERIC BENTLEY

Fɪʀsᴛ published in 1953, *In Search of Theater* is widely regarded as the standard portrait of the European and American theatre in the turbulent and seminal years following World War II. The book's influence contributed substantially to the rising reputations of such artists as Bertolt Brecht, Charles Chaplin and Martha Graham.

"The most erudite and intelligent living writer on the theatre."

—Ronald Bryden, *The New Statesman*

"Cᴇʀᴛᴀɪɴʟʏ Aᴍᴇʀɪᴄᴀ's ғᴏʀᴇᴍᴏsᴛ ᴛʜᴇᴀᴛʀᴇ ᴄʀɪᴛɪᴄ..."

—Irving Wardle, *The Times*

ISBN: 1-55783-111-4

APPLAUSE

THE MADMAN AND THE NUN and THE CRAZY LOCOMOTIVE

THREE PLAYS (including THE WATER HEN)

by Stanislaw Ignacy Witkiewicz

Edited, translated and with an introduction by Daniel Gerould and C. S. Durer

Foreword by Jan Kott

"It is high time that this major playwright should become better known in the English-speaking world."
—Martin Esslin

STARTLING discontinuities and surprises erupt throughout these avant-garde landscapes by Poland's outstanding modern dramatist. A decadent poet rebels against society's repressive tyranny through suicide and last minute resurrection in *Madman and the Nun*. A band of degenerate criminals and artists in *The Crazy Locomotive* commandeer an engine and seek to bring about God's judgment by racing at apocalyptic speeds into an oncoming passenger train. Painter, photographer, novelist, philosopher, expert on drugs, Witkiewicz exemplifies in these dramas his mastery of a new art of the theatre.

ISBN: 0-936839-83-X

APPLAUSE